C000092447

Access to Higher —
The Unfinished Business

edited by
Liz Thomas, Michael Cooper
& Jocey Quinn

EUROPEAN ACCESS NETWORK

Acknowledgements

The editors would like to thank members of the Institute for Access Studies at Staffordshire University for providing editorial support, and all the contributors who have patiently fulfilled the editors' requests in the preparation of the chapters for this book.

The editors would also like to thank the European Access Network (EAN), especially Maggie Woodrow and Professor Dr Dario Villannueva Prieto, for organising the 9th EAN Annual Convention, September 2000, Santiago de Compostela, Spain.

Published by
The Institute for Access Studies, Staffordshire University
&
European Access Network

First published 2001

ISBN 1 8978989 40

Design, layout and setting
by Carmel Dennison

Printed in Great Britain
by Stowes the Printer, Longton, Stoke-on-Trent

Access to Higher Education:
The Unfinished Business

Contents

Notes on the Contributors

Eugene L. Anderson is currently a doctoral candidate in the Department of Educational Policy Studies at the University of Virginia. He holds a Bachelor of Arts in African-American Studies from the University of Pennsylvania, and a Master of Urban Planning from the University of Virginia. His areas of interest are higher education policy, intercollegiate athletics, and urban planning. He has worked with numerous community development organisations in both Philadelphia and Charlottesville, Virginia.

Julie Ann Andreshak is a graduate student at the University of Minnesota, pursuing a Ph.D. degree in Comparative and International Development Education in the Department of Educational Policy and Administration, where she is a graduate assistant. Previously, she served two years in the United States Peace Corps in Morocco. She earned her MA and BA degrees at the University of Wisconsin-Milwaukee in Curriculum & Instruction in ESL and International Relations, respectively.

Derek Bland has worked in the education sector since graduating in 1981 with qualifications in art and secondary teaching. After spending some time in teaching and school improvement (through the Disadvantaged Schools Programme), he joined the staff of Queensland University of Technology in Brisbane. Since 1991, he has coordinated the university's special entry and support programme (Q-Step) for students from socio-economically disadvantaged backgrounds.

Judith Brooks-Buck is a former Executive Director of the NOAH Group, L.L.C., a company whose mission is to help disenfranchised individuals become self-sufficient. In her current role, she is principal author of Community and Supportive Service Work Plans, required by the U.S. Department of Housing and Urban Development (HUD) during the grant application process. She is also responsible for research, development, and design of educational programmes for NOAH's nation-wide self-sufficiency network. She has years of experience as an educator, former Housing Authority Commissioner, programme director, national and international presenter, and author. She has presented and published articles in many fields relating to education. She is currently a Doctoral Candidate at the University of Virginia with research efforts focused on educational policy, and politics.

Michael Cooper is director of the International Office at Karlstad University, Sweden. He holds a degree in modern languages from King's College London and a research degree in

English from Göteborg University, Sweden. Previously he was head of the School of Modern Languages at Karlstad where he lectured in English, in particular language and linguistics. Among his many other activities, he is currently President of the Compostela Group of Universities and a member of the committee of the European Access Network. He has worked extensively as a translator and language editor of scientific publications.

Gaie Davidson-Burnet joined the Department of Research & Statistics at UCAS in 1995 from the University of Kent at Canterbury, where she held the post of Senior Research Fellow in the School of Continuing Education. Prior to the five years she spent at Kent, Gaie was a Senior Lecturer for twelve years in the Department of Government and Political Science at London Guildhall University. Her main concerns throughout her career have been the inequities of higher educational opportunities and she has spent many years researching and writing in the field of access, flexible credit systems and work-based learning.

Fran Ferrier is a Research Fellow in the ACER Centre for the Economics of Education and Training, at Monash University in Australia. Fran has many years experience in policy-related research in higher and vocational education with particular interests in intellectual capital management, innovation, and equity and diversity issues.

Robin Gutteridge has a keen interest in promoting social justice. Her academic background and interest is the application of psychology and sociology to health care and she is especially interested in the relevance of life course development theories to continuing personal and professional development. Sh e became interested in access issues through teaching, through working with people with disabilities and through an advice and guidance role with the Open University. She has continued to develop her interests as Admissions Tutor for the BSc Physiotherapy programme at Coventry University and through her work as liaison tutor for physiotherapy students with additional needs. Currently she is writing up her PhD, which is grounded in life course development theory.

Zubaida Hague is a research fellow working on a project aiming to identify the main determinants of degree performances and first destinations of work for graduates. She has researched and written extensively on social, economic and public policy matters relating to minority ethnic communities, and more recently helped to draft a report for the Commission on the Future of Multi-ethnic Britain. Zubaida has a doctorate in Education (explaining the performances of Bangladeshi pupils in British secondary schools) and has extended her interest into employment and labour market areas.

Margaret Heagney is Student Equity Officer in the Student Equity and Access Branch of Monash University, Australia. She has participated in a number of collaborative research projects in the UK and Europe and has presented to the Australian Research Council and the HE Council on student issues.

Anthony Heywood is course leader of the part-time BA(Hons) Fine Art at the Kent Institute of Art & Design. He exhibits in America, Britain and the Netherlands, and coordinates the PARC Public Art Research Centre at Canterbury. He is a Senior Research Fellow of KIAD. His studio is based near Canterbury and he is presently exhibiting in the London Bienalle and Pardo Gallery, New York, USA.

Kate Hughes teaches cultural studies on the part-time BA in Fine Art at Canterbury. She has contributed to a number of exhibition catalogues and has written extensively on both the development of higher education in Cyprus and its effects on women. She is a regular contributor to the THES.

Elizabeth Peters joined the Department of Research & Statistics at UCAS in January 1997 after holding the post of Computer Manager at the Art and Design Admissions Registry (ADAR) since 1992. She has the key role of overseeing the collection of access course data for the database of courses that form the Schedule 2 list for approval by the Government, and works closely with the Quality Assurance Agency who have responsibility for validating access courses. In addition to her access course role, she also provides support for the three elements of the Forecasting & Planning Service: the Institutional Planning Service, the Applicant Postcode Tracking Service and the Forecasting Service.

Ellen Piesanen works as a senior researcher at the Institute for Educational Research in the University of Jyväskylä, Finland. Her research area concerns higher education, especially Finnish Open University and the Lifelong Learning.

Devi Rajab is Dean of Student Development at the University of Natal. A psychologist by training, Devi has several publications in international and local journals on women's issues, prejudice and intergroup relations, and serves on several boards in community and educational organisations. She sees her role in South Africa as offering training and development towards community and nation building, with particular emphasis on life-skills, cultural diversity and enhancing intergroup relations and gender issues with regard to empowering women and promoting harmonious gender relations within the family.

Maria San-Segundo has been Associate Professor at the University of the Basque Country (Bilbao) and at the University Carlos III of Madrid. Between 1994 and 1996 she was advisor to the Secretary of State for Universities and Research (Ministry of Education). She is currently Vice-Rector in charge of access at the University Carlos III, and has been appointed by the Spanish Parliament as member of the Council of Universities. Maria San-Segundo has published more than 60 papers in Spanish and international journals, dealing with the efficiency of educational systems, equality of opportunities, economic returns to human capital, financing policies and regional inequalities in human capital.

Kim Slack is a research officer in the Institute for Access Studies at Staffordshire University in the UK. Having entered higher education as a mature student via an access course, she has a personal as well as a professional interest in the field. Kim is currently engaged in evaluation research on a number of projects aimed at widening participation in post-16 education amongst non-traditional learners, in particular working with young people in schools from the age of five years.

Jan Smith is a lecturer in post-compulsory education and education management at Sheffield Hallam University, and has carried out research into aspects of student experience in further and higher education. She has previously worked in community, adult and further education, and as an adviser in post-16 education. She is currently acting as coordinator for a regional widening participation project led by Sheffield Hallam University

Liz Thomas is a senior research fellow and director of the Institute for Access Studies at Staffordshire University in the UK. The Institute for Access Studies is a research centre dedicated to widening participation, lifelong learning and social inclusion. Liz has a long-standing interest in evaluation and social policy, as this was the focus of her PhD at the University of Sheffield. She is currently engaged in academic and evaluation research in the field of widening participation in post-compulsory education.

Sue Webb is a senior lecturer and director of the Institute for Lifelong Learning in the School of Education at the University of Sheffield in the UK Currently, the Institute has a number of specific widening participation projects in, community work skills (European Union funded) and flexible learning (HEFCE funded) and is engaged in research and evaluation in lifelong learning. She has undertaken a number of research projects on access and alternative entry to higher education and is interested in education policy analysis and in exploring learner identities and experiences.

Introduction

Michael Cooper

As we move into the twenty-first century, education and in particular higher education, is assuming an increasingly important role in, on the one hand, empowering individuals to claim their rightful place in society and, on the other, providing society with the more highly educated and qualified workforce it needs to handle the technologically ever more complex nature of work. However, there are still large groups of citizens, even in the industrialised nations, who for one reason or another do not have access to educational opportunities and thus risk exclusion. Much has been said and done to foster mass education but the fact still remains that in many countries with compulsory, state-provided basic education, many individuals leave school without full command of fundamental literacy and numeracy. Many others terminate their formal, and even informal, education after compulsory school to seek employment in the shrinking market of unskilled and semi-skilled jobs. The obstacles to continuing one's education and accessing higher levels are many; they are both external and internal; external in the sense that society or geography have created barriers in the form, for instance, of race, gender, religion or location; internal in a psychological sense that individuals raise their own barriers against pursuing their education. Even in the latter case, society may be said to have failed the individual in not providing the necessary help and stimulus to overcome the psychological obstacles. Nevertheless, whatever the reason, the result is the same – exclusion.

This present volume is an attempt to assess where we stand today, primarily as regards access to higher education, defined as 'post-secondary'. The chapters present a wide range of perspectives on the issue of access, moving from a consideration of general trends over an assessment of national trends in a number of countries to a discussion of specific discourses and initiatives. The authors are mainly academics and practitioners and come from all parts of the globe. Access issues differ in degree in different countries, in some places it being a matter of providing basic education to all, whereas in others there are more specific issues that have to be considered. However, the fundamental discourse is similar – what has been and is being done to remove the obstacles to access to higher education and how successful this has been.

Maria San Segundo provides an historical overview, which briefly summarises some of the changes that have come about in higher education in OECD countries during the 20th

1

century, with particular regard to access. Her objective is to evaluate the current situation and to identify the issues that still need to be resolved in order to achieve equal opportunity of access. Her discussion concentrates on three major changes

(1) The expansion and changing role of higher education
(2) Equality of opportunity in education
(3) Lifelong learning

She concludes that we have seen an unprecedented expansion of higher education and that the transition from elite to mass higher education has brought about many changes. The massive access of women to higher education has played a crucial role in the general expansion. However, it is only in the developed world that the presence of women is greater than that of men. Using statistics, she demonstrates that the probability of reaching the tertiary level is clearly related to the socio-economic status of the family. Her final point is that the challenge of lifelong learning to higher education may require organisational changes as well as innovative financial policies in order to address the needs of different groups of adults.

In the second chapter, Mary-Louise Kearney sets the contemporary scene, taking as her point of departure article 3a of the World Conference on Higher Education Declaration from 1998 that "no discrimination can be accepted in granting access to higher education on grounds of race, gender, language or religion, or economic, cultural or social distinctions, or physical disabilities". She provides a thorough overview of the steps that have been taken since then at the global level and how educational providers have responded, considering in particular the reality of wider access and the lessons that have been learnt. Special attention is given to the importance of the availability of lifelong learning and the gravity of the inequality of access to technology. The chapter concludes that we must recognise the enormous opportunities that are available and that higher or tertiary education must demonstrate its commitment to three major objectives:

• promoting all citizens' participation in development;
• reinforcing the learning society;
• ensuring the quality and relevance of the new order.

With these two chapters as a general background, the next four chapters concentrate on national progress with the first two focusing on the UK, the third on Finland and the fourth on South Africa. In their chapter, Gaie Davidson-Burnet and Liz Peters examine the tripartite Forecasting & Planning Service, designed by the Department of Research & Statistics at the Universities and Colleges Admission Service (UCAS) to support universities and colleges in identifying groups of students who are underrepresented within their establishment and in supporting their initiatives to widen access. Having first outlined the three services offered: the Institutional Planning Service, Applicant Postcode Tracking Service, and Forecasting Service, the chapter goes on to present a survey of fifty institutions and sector bodies exploring their knowledge and usage of the services. The authors conclude their discussion by highlighting a number of issues which both institutions and UCAS might address if, together, they wish to tackle the issue of widening access to categories of people currently underrepresented in higher educational establishments in the UK.

Jan Smith's contribution concentrates on evaluation as such using the term to refer to any strategy for assessing progress. She makes some very pertinent comments about traditional ways of assessing widening participation activities, which often resort to either number crunching or case studies and do not really tell us anything. She argues that evaluation of access initiatives poses some special problems. The nature of the work does not easily lend itself to short-term measurement or to organisational quality systems. Many activities and projects are developmental and innovative and many are community-based, so that reconciling different interests is challenging. Given this, she uses her recent experience in a research project in the United Kingdom, the UK policy context, and literature on evaluation, to propose a framework for planning evaluations, based on six 'key dimensions'. The framework does not detail methods but underlines the crucial role of evaluation in highlighting issues and effecting change. The chapter concludes with a comment on the need for more research on certain aspects of widening participation and also underlines the value of sharing practice.

Ellen Piesanen's article discusses the role of Finnish summer universities operating as part of the Finnish educational system to improve the preconditions for lifelong learning at the regional level. They deliver, on the one hand, open university instruction that accords with the degree requirements of the regular universities and, on the other hand, liberal adult education as well as vocational courses, lectures for the third age, Studia Generalia lectures, seminars and various local-level cultural events. Although operating at a regional level, their catchment areas cover the whole of Finland. The courses are open to all, irrespective of age and previous education. In a sparsely populated country they are an important factor in promoting educational equality. Their operational model is flexible and involves a minimum of organisational structures, which enables them to offer an extensive and varied range of teaching. As a result, they can cater for a very diverse range of clients, including groups with access to little or no other educational provision, and also those at risk of marginalisation, such as the unemployed, people with inadequate basic education and immigrants.

Whereas Finland has a long tradition of democracy, which is an absolute prerequisite for any efforts to achieve equal opportunity and equal access in education, South Africa only recently started along this path. As Devi Rajab observes in her contribution, South African constitutions, prior to the new democratic dispensation, were premised on inequality and steadfast commitment to white supremacy. The apartheid policy in law and application systematically discriminated against black people in all aspects of social and educational life. The end result is, as she demonstrates, a society where inequality is one of the defining characteristics. In the light of this, South Africa's smooth transition into a non-racist democracy has been hailed widely as nothing short of a miracle.

With these facts as a background, Devi Rajab discusses the transformation of higher education in South Africa, what this requires from the government and from the institutions of higher education, how the problem of student diversity, in the form of ethnic background, basic education, financial situation etc, is to be addressed and what the role of higher education should be in nation-building. She points out that several partnership initiatives are underway involving civil society, government, business and higher education and concludes that the main task of education planners and policy makers has been to change the education and training system in South Africa bringing it in line with international trends. The core values and principles of higher education as advanced in the Education White Paper 3: A programme for transforming higher education 1997 are equity and redress, quality, development, effectiveness and efficiency. The challenge to higher education in South Africa lies in developing a synchronicity between the forces of globalisation, international trends and local demands.

These national assessments are followed by a number of specific access discourses, the title of the first of which, "disadvantage is complex" could stand as a motto for the whole volume. Here Fran Ferrier and Margaret Heagney examine some of the strengths and weaknesses of the Australian model of targeting special groups selected on the basis of particular social and economic characteristics as the primary approach to dealing with inequities in education at all

4

levels. The comments and arguments the authors present draw on the research of many people who have contributed to advances in the understanding of educational disadvantage in Australia and on the experience of a project they undertook at Monash University, which emphasised the complex reality of disadvantage, and the inability of the target group approach to address this reality by itself. Although their findings do not lead them to advocate an end to selecting particular target groups for support, they maintain that the disadvantage that some people face in entering, participating, completing and gaining successful outcomes from education is dynamic rather than static, and complex rather than simple and that a focus on target groups by itself is inadequate to counter their difficulties and achieve equity for all.

In her contribution, Julie Ann Andreshak turns her attention once again to the UK and considers the vexed issue of university funding and tuition fees. She analyses the policy of introducing tuition fees in higher education in the UK in the late 90s and, within a larger framework of political and economic changes, examines the theoretical reasoning underpinning the reform as well as empirical evidence used to support the reform in light of potential impacts on access to underrepresented groups. Her conclusions are that the trend towards market-driven higher education is likely to continue. These mechanisms have the potential to augment efficiency and quality but may have negative effects on equity. However, she points out that the commitment of government to fund students following the 1963 Robbins Report did not substantially increase participation from less represented groups. Thus, tuition issues alone are not a sufficient explanation for access problems. She believes that access to higher education has the potential to increase even with this reform in place if currently underrepresented students are actively recruited. The key to making certain that access is not impeded by funding measures requires that 1) further research is conducted in order to reveal how funding policies impact a student's decision to (or not to) participate in higher education; and 2) attention be paid to the issues that contribute to the rest of the explanation behind limits on access.

Zubaida Hague argues that British universities have had some success in increasing the participation of students from minority ethnic backgrounds, although problems relating to gender proportions within some ethnic groups still remain. Poor representation of students from deprived socio-economic backgrounds also continues to be a major problem within British universities, with little evidence nationally to indicate any significant improvement in access. Her chapter discusses some of the findings relating to ethnic and social class participation across UK universities, but concentrates on the more important question of what happens to these students in the period between their entering university and leaving it. Using data on over 2,000 university students, she evaluates the progress (retention rates) and final achievements of different ethnic and social class groups in one inner city university, and attempts to explain the nature of the disadvantages that some of these groups may be experiencing at university. The analysis presents a complex picture, with differences between ethnic, social class, gender and age groups in many of the areas being taken into account. Her most important conclusion is perhaps that universities need a more critical approach to the subject, one that allows for variation *within* groups as well as *between* groups, to identify who the 'underrepresented' and 'disadvantaged' groups in relation to higher education are. Universities need research to help them understand why particular groups are disadvantaged and how they can assist these groups in overcoming their disadvantages.

Judith Brooks-Buck and Eugene L. Anderson examine a very different topic in their extremely interesting and illuminative chapter: African-American access to higher education through athletics, a topic which has remained controversial since the first athletes of colour were allowed to compete at collegiate level. Whereas athletic scholarships give talented African-American students an opportunity to access a college education, which they otherwise would not have had, the authors show that the graduation rates for these students are significantly lower than the average for student athletes. Thus they argue that the scholarships are somewhat of a double-edged sword. They are attractive to students because they see that top level athletes are regarded as heroes, and they are attractive to the students' parents as a pathway to a college degree and thus entry into mainstream society, since uneducated Africa-Americans can hardly compete in a culture that values education, and gaining access and completing a degree programme is an essential passport. However, because of the demands of top-level college sports and the lack of support from the college, many of the students fail to obtain their degree. The chapter thus raises the issue of whether African-American athletes are given a gift when awarded scholarships to prestigious universities or simply used as cheap labour. This thought-provoking contribution concludes with the hope that some combination of success for both the institutions and a representative portion of the individual athletes may become a reality one day.

The complexity of widening participation is highlighted once again in Robin Gutteridge's contribution, a discourse which concentrates on the importance of addressing social and individual life course issues. Her study, which draws on a number of years' experience of work in widening access and retention, on published and unpublished work, expert opinion and work in progress, proposes that the existence of core skills of communication, self management and self appraisal may be predictors of successful participation equal to academic attainment, especially in underrepresented groups. Using evidence from admission and from interventions to support students with additional needs, she concludes that student support or progress in higher education cannot be seen in isolation from the social context, both organisational and individual, and that the effect of previous experience must be taken into account. Advice, guidance and strategies to widen participation are integral to retention but successful strategies for widening participation need to take account of the life skills on entry and incorporate planned continuing development.

Information technology skills have become a new form of literacy for the 21st century, and the development of IT-based learning and teaching has been promoted as a key strategy to widen access to learning opportunities. The Higher Education Funding Council for England, for example, in many of its recent special funded initiatives in widening participation, identifies the role of web-based information in raising aspirations and encouraging the participation of those who are underrepresented in higher education. However, Sue Webb shows that the impact of new technologies on the learning of currently excluded groups has been woefully underexplored. She argues that 'technological fixes' will solve some problems, but others of cost and accessibility are likely to remain. Social divisions do not disappear in virtual environments, they merely take on a new form. The premise that new learning technologies promote social inclusion is still relatively untested, though the discourses of policy makers and IT enthusiasts claim otherwise. Her contribution examines these competing claims and the mechanisms by which discourses of new technologies in education have been constructed. Given the widespread belief that IT is the panacea for all evils, her work provides some refreshingly balanced insights.

The Institute for Access Studies at Staffordshire University is involved in research to evaluate initiatives that aim to widen participation and promote lifelong learning amongst underrepresented groups. Liz Thomas and Kim Slack draw on this research, presenting two case studies of strategies to promote lifelong learning amongst adults who have not previously participated in formal post-compulsory learning. One is a community-based initiative involving further education colleges and education community link workers. The second case study is a work-based scheme, offering NVQs (National Vocational Qualifications assessed via a portfolio of work demonstrating competencies) to non-teaching staff in schools. These staff are primarily parents (usually women), who are employed in part-time, low-paid work as lunch time supervisors and classroom assistants and who would not otherwise participate in lifelong learning. Drawing on a comparison of the initiatives, the authors use a grounded theory approach to develop an evaluation framework for assessing the contribution of different approaches to promote lifelong learning amongst educationally marginalised adults.

Another interesting specific initiative is the Q-Step Programme at Queensland University of Technology, a programme intended to promote and assist entrance to tertiary education for students from low socio-economic backgrounds. Derek Bland reports on an unplanned but very welcome outcome of the programme, the election of a group of Q-Step students to key positions in the Student Guild (Union) in 2000. His article is a case study of work-in-progress, looking at the steps towards empowerment that have led to a situation where a group of five non-traditional students have come to represent the mainstream student body in the arena of student politics. It examines the role played by the Q-Step Programme and the major influences on the students. It also considers the flow-on this may have to prospective students of similar background with whom the group has contact. Q-Step's safety net of support services recognises the need for commencing tertiary students to establish strong peer networks and to find their niche within the institution as a prerequisite to success. Many non-traditional students commence tertiary study feeling disempowered and isolated, so Q-Step's on-campus support starts with a targeted orientation programme and includes a peer support association. This appears not only to have helped to overcome the problem of alienation for this group, but also to have encouraged them to take up student leadership roles within the university.

The final chapter is a presentation of an exciting initiative in the field of widening participation, a case study of a specialised degree programme in Fine Art. This particular programme is part time, and was set up, over ten years ago, in the Kent Institute of Art and Design to specifically increase the participation of mature students previously denied educational opportunity. In their study, Kate Hughes and Anthony Heywood briefly outline the history of part-time degree provision in Britain, and then examine the anomalies that exist in fine art education. These are principally that it does not have an immediately obvious commercial application and that it is frequently regarded as elitist. The authors describe how marketing, collaboration, learning support and curriculum delivery have all evolved to help dispel these notions, and also meet the very particular needs of widely diverse students. Besides examining these changes, their outcomes and how future policy should proceed, the chapter also includes a brief study of added value. Each cohort was divided into qualified and unqualified at the point of entry and then degree classifications compared. The conclusion summarises the contribution the programme has made to lifelong learning, underlining the danger lurking in a society which prioritises immediate commercial application and neglects the freedom to explore knowledge. Much has been achieved, say the authors, but we still have a long way to go.

In some sense this might be a general conclusion we could draw from the whole set of articles included in this volume. However, having surveyed the plethora of initiatives and actions that have been implemented to widen participation and to stimulate retention, and the research that is being conducted in the field, one cannot but be impressed by what has been achieved. Our knowledge and, perhaps above all, our will to assist non-traditional and disadvantaged groups gain access to higher education are much greater today at the turn of the millennium than a mere decade ago. The most encouraging sign is the change of attitude that is taking place, the growing belief that institutions of higher education have to change to accommodate other groups. A factor that should not be neglected in this context is funding. In many of the developed countries the age cohorts of traditional university students are declining and university managements are realising that they need to look to a wider range of students to maintain funding levels. Necessity, indeed, is the mother of invention. It is our hope that the present volume represents a small contribution to this process.

Karlstad
May, 2001

Chapter One

Access in the OECD: the unfinished business of the 20th century

María San Segundo

Introduction

This chapter briefly summarises some of the changes that have come about in higher education during the 20th century, paying special attention to the three aspects that have had the greatest influence on the access of the population in general to this level of education. The objective of this analysis is two fold. On the one hand, to evaluate the current situation regarding the presence of different social groups in higher education. On the other hand, to identify the issues that still present a challenge in order to reach equal opportunities of access, and graduation, in higher education in the 21st century.

Access to higher education in the 20th century

If we consider the changes that have taken place in higher education over the 20th century, we could mention many academic, scientific, social, cultural or financial aspects that have suffered profound transformations. Here, however, I shall only consider three important changes that may influence the evolution of higher education in the coming century. They are the following:

(1) The expansion and changing role of higher education
(2) Equality of opportunity in education
(3) Lifelong learning

I shall look at the impact of each of them on recent reforms and on the challenges for higher education in the future.

The expansion and changing role of higher education

The tertiary level of the education system has undergone an unprecedented expansion over the 20th century, especially since the 1950s. This expansion is usually summarised by the idea that higher education no longer serves to educate an elite, but has become a tool for educating the masses. This process of growth came about in particular after the Second World War with the economic growth that a great number of countries experienced. The rising standard of living per capita was accompanied by social, cultural and political changes which favoured the access to higher education of a wide spectrum of the population in both developed countries and some developing countries.

With this growth came a change in the social perception of the role of higher education, as well as important reforms in the organisation and the curriculum of study programmes. There was resistance to these reforms which caused conflicts, especially in the universities, which passed from the education of a social and intellectual minority in a reduced number of disciplines, to a much wider spectrum of tasks. Besides creating and transmitting knowledge, they had to train professionals of differing areas, encourage local economic growth, promote social mobility, participate in democratic development and spread cultural knowledge (UNESCO, 1991). In order to try to cover these functions there was a great diversification in both study programmes and institutions that tried to provide a service to an ever more numerous and heterogeneous clientele. No longer is it possible to consider only the traditional student: young people who have recently left secondary education and who can dedicate themselves full time to education. Now, a large percentage of those entering higher education (OECD, 2000) are adult students, with very diverse previous training, who study part time or follow distance learning courses. The heterogeneous nature of the students, the changes in the production system and the new technologies will continue to bring about further changes to higher education in the new millennium.

Figure 1

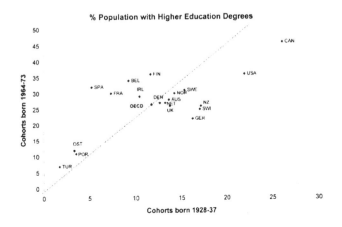

% Population with Higher Education Degrees

11

In figure 1 the magnitude of the expansion can be seen by comparing the levels of human capital in the generations born between 1928 and 1937 with those reached by individuals born between 1964 and 1973, for the OECD countries. In the generations of the 1930s, only 12% of the population obtained a degree, whereas, in the second group this percentage has risen to 26% on average in OECD countries.

The growth in general is important, but the individual evolution of the twenty countries considered varies. There is a group of countries that are above the average in both periods: The United States and Canada form the leading group, and are followed by Norway, Sweden and Australia. Of the countries that were below average in the first period and above average in the second, we can mention five European countries: Finland, Belgium, Spain, France and Ireland, that show very considerable growth.

Figures 2 and 3

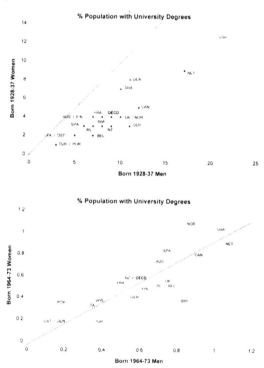

It is a well known fact that the general expansion in higher education over the last forty years is due to the incorporation of women to all levels of education. The magnitude of the change can be seen in figures 2 and 3 when we compare the situation of men and women in the above mentioned generations. For the population born between 1928 and 1937 access to higher education was greater for men than for women in each and every one of the 20 countries analysed[1]. The average for the OECD corresponds to a masculine rate of higher degrees that is double the feminine rate (9% versus 4%).

The situation had changed drastically for the population born between 1964 and 1973, since almost all the countries show a situation of equality between the sexes. The average percentage of graduates reaches 16% for both men and women. The only noticeable exceptions from the state of general equilibrium are Switzerland (9 points in favour of the men), and Norway and Spain (6 points in favour of the women). This evolution of women's participation in higher education, in the context of the OECD, probably explains why not one single paper dealing with an analysis of the access of women to higher education was presented to the 2000 EAN conference. This fact is a reflection of the great advance that has been achieved in this field, even though we all know that inequalities persist where certain areas of education are concerned, such as, for example, the technical subjects. Many of us will doubtless continue to work in this area over the next few years. It would seem evident that massive access by women to higher education both accompanies and plays an important role in many of the most important social changes that have taken place in the 20th century. It is one of the most outstanding aspects of the equal opportunities policy of recent decades, at least in developed countries.

However, we should remember that the situation of women in the education system is not the same in other parts of the world. Thus, in figure 4 it can be seen how, in various parts of Asia or Africa, the participation of men in higher education is much higher than that of women[2]. Only in the developed world is the presence of women greater than that of men (by a small margin), while Latin America comes close to achieving this. It is reasonable to suppose that if this meeting was not concentrating on OECD countries, then the analysis of the access of people of different sexes would be a very important theme in the sessions. Equal opportunities for men and women is far from being a reality in most parts of the world and makes the list of questions pending for the new millennium even longer.

Figure 4

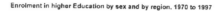

Enrolment in higher Education by sex and by region, 1970 to 1997

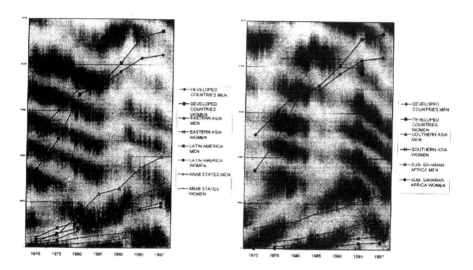

Equality of opportunity in education

Nevertheless, the search for equality in education has not been limited to combating the existing inequalities between individuals of differing sex, race, age or socioeconomic origin. In addition, such policies as there are are not limited to the tertiary level, but include the whole education system, giving special attention to the obligatory stages that the whole population must pass through. The idea of equal opportunities in education today is, in principle, accepted by almost all countries. This fact is reflected in the Universal Declaration of Human Rights of 1948, as well as in the Convention against discrimination in education of 1960. Equal opportunities in education has recently become an important goal of social policy. The reduction of inequalities has been a goal of the education systems in the second half of the 20th century. However, the notion of equal opportunities has been developing and evolving along with the expansion in education that has been taking place since the 19th century. The spread of state education, the consolidation of obligatory education and the civil rights movements are three factors that have had an important influence on policies of equality in education (Coleman, 1968).

With the industrial revolution and the development of the market economy, state education, open to children of all social classes, began to take on relevance in the 19th century, especially in the USA where the population is integrated in state schools with a common curriculum. In some European countries, on the other hand, a more stratified system is maintained, with a very strong private sector providing education to the better off social classes. In addition, various curricula are developed that, from an early age, condition the future work prospects of the young people. Many of these tensions between state and private education, and between a common curriculum or diversified programs are still evident today (Levin, 1983). However, at the end of the 19th century, we can say that, in the developed countries, primary and secondary education covered practically the whole population, and that it was mainly imparted in state schools where comprehensive programs predominate (OECD, 2000). The equal opportunities policy is based on these characteristics of the education system and is complemented by the programmes of grants and compensatory education. Historically, there has been a tendency to consider that public finance, in general, guarantees the equality of resources and quality of the centres. This supposition began to be questioned seriously in the USA in the 60s and 70s, and today it is the object of debate in almost every country. Thus, interest in evaluating the quality of different educational centres has grown noticeably in the last fifteen years (OECD, 1998a).

The publication of the famous report (Coleman *et al.*, 1966) on 'Equal Opportunities in Education' can be considered as the starting point of this public debate on quality in education and what is necessary to achieve it[3]. The Coleman report analyses the inequalities existing between the educational input and output of different centres and groups of students in the USA. Its conclusions had a widespread effect on the educational debates, and put a great emphasis on the importance of the socio-economic origin of the students, as well as of the characteristics of their classmates (the so-called 'peergroup effects'), as an influence on the academic achievement. These results, and others from research carried out by psychologists, also had a great impact on the policy of breaking with racial segregation in schools. It could be interpreted that the Coleman Report gave some support to the Supreme Court's sentence in the Brown case. This sentence put an end in 1945 to the doctrine of 'Separate but Equal', giving rise to integrated schools where black and white students shared the same classrooms.

The acceptance of the goal of equal opportunities, as well as the stimulus of multidisciplinary research (from sociology, pedagogy, psychology and economics) on how to achieve it effectively, both had a notable impact on the formulation of policies in higher education too. The recognition of equal rights of access for the whole population is usually complemented by a policy of financial help which tries to eliminate the dependence on investment in education with respect to the family's socio-economic origin. Recently, education systems and their centres have concentrated on analysing academic performance, trying to achieve equal opportunities of graduation for students from different backgrounds.

Figure 5

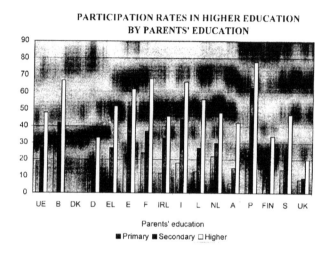

PARTICIPATION RATES IN HIGHER EDUCATION
BY PARENTS' EDUCATION

Parents' education
■ Primary ■ Secondary □ Higher

However, the available data shows that higher education has still not managed to offer equal opportunities of access and graduation to individuals. Figure 5 illustrates some of the challenges still to be met in developed countries to reduce the existing ratio between access to higher education and the socio-economic level of the family. The data gathered by Eurostat proves that in 1997 the probability of reaching the tertiary level is over 60% in Portugal, France, Spain, Italy and Belgium, for young people whose parents have a degree. In another six countries the figure is over 40%. On the other hand, among students whose parents did not finish secondary school, the probability of access to higher education does not reach 20% in Ireland, Greece, Italy, Germany, Austria, Finland, Sweden, Luxembourg and the United Kingdom. In the other five countries analysed, the probability hardly surpassed 20%. The inequalities of schooling according to socio-economic level are thus common to all the developed countries[4], and make up part of the agenda for the next century.

Lifelong learning

In the nineties' a consensus was reached concerning the importance of promoting individuals' access to lifelong learning.

- To satisfy the needs of continuous formation which allow knowledge and abilities to be brought up to date, as well as the recycling of workers.

- For socio-cultural reasons such as greater life expectancy and improved standards of living which lead to a greater demand for training.

The rapid changes that have taken place over the last few decades in the labour market show the wholesale need for lifelong learning. As a consequence of technical change and international competition between different countries and economic areas, workers need to be recycled and gain further qualifications in order to adapt to new jobs. Thus, higher education institutions do not only provide initial formation, but increasingly provide continuous formation. 'Access' to higher education can occur several times throughout a person's lifetime, to carry out studies, sometimes general and sometimes specialised; sometimes over a long period of time and sometimes for only a few weeks.

The idea of training throughout one's life therefore demands that the higher education system be more flexible. Moreover, as pointed out by the OECD, the new goals in education for the whole population place the student, and their needs, centre stage. The education and training systems need to be oriented towards 'The demand side rather than the supply side of the educational market' (OECD, 1998b). The fundamental goal must be to teach how to learn so that adults can deal with the differing training needs, with updating and renewing qualifications. It seems clear that the lifelong learning approach affects the whole educational system, and especially higher education. Its prominent position on the frontier of knowledge gives it a crucial role in the updating of the formation of the best qualified human capital.

Education policy also faces important challenges that institutions cannot always solve by themselves. Thus, for example, encouraging lifelong learning may require the use of programmes of student financial aid, both complex and diversified. Many educational systems have traditionally excluded adults from their programmes of grants and loans, considering that they are capable of financing investment in their own formation. However, problems arise not only due to the limited ability to pay of many families with children in schooling ages, but also due to the uncertain economic performance of the educational investment of adults.

As they are closer to the end of their working life than young people, there is less time to profit from their investment by way of salary[6]. However, the social benefits may be appreciable as the probability of becoming unemployed is reduced, social security payments increase as well as taxes to be paid in the future, and even include the benefits that children may reap from the increase in the family's human capital. It would seem there is a need to do more research into all the private and social benefits in order to be able to formulate a policy to finance lifelong learning which favours efficiency and equality.

With the data available today concerning the education of adults, there seems to be some reason for concern about the growth of inequalities between countries. Thus, in figure 6, it can be seen that the rates of enrolment for the population between 30 and 39 years of age differ greatly among the developed countries. The influence of income per capita seems to be important, so the bottom places are taken by the Czech Republic, Turkey, Poland, Hungary, Spain and Ireland, although they are joined by two richer countries, Italy and France, which have not encouraged adult education. Outstanding in this field are the cases of Australia and Sweden, followed by the United Kingdom, New Zealand and Finland. In 1998 these five countries reached levels of participation in education of the population between 30 and 39 years of age above the average for the OECD countries, and above the place that could correspond to them due to income level. The OECD data also suggests that part-time education has a notable presence in these countries, a fact that may help to explain their success with the access of adults to education. Without a doubt, these countries deserve a detailed analysis in order to identify cases of good practice that may be useful for other educational systems.

Conclusions

The 20th century has known an unprecedented expansion of higher education. The transition from elite to mass higher education has brought about many changes. This chapter summarises some of the main transformations. Using recent OECD statistics, the magnitude of the expansion in tertiary graduates is evaluated. Among the population cohorts born in the 1930s, only 12 % obtained a degree. For the generations born in the late sixties this percentage rises to 26 % in the OECD.

Massive access of women to higher education plays a crucial role in the general expansion. However, it is shown that only in the developed word is the presence of women greater than that of men. Equal opportunities for men and women is far from being a reality in most parts of the world and makes the list of questions pending for the new millennium even longer.

In the second half of the 20th century countries have adopted the goal of equal opportunities in education. However, the data available shows that higher education has not managed to offer equal opportunities of access to individuals even in the more developed countries. Using Eurostat data, it is shown that the probability of reaching the tertiary level is clearly related to the socioeconomic status of the family. Breaking this relationship is one of the challenges left for the 21st century.

Lastly, the importance of lifelong learning is highlighted. Higher education should play a crucial role in its promotion. However this new challenge for the tertiary level may require important organisational changes as well as innovative financial policies in order to address the needs of different groups of adults.

References

Chapman, B. (1997). "Conceptual issues and the Australian experience with income contingent charges for Higher Education", *The Economic Journal*, n° 107, pp. 738-751.

Coleman, J. et al (1966). *Equality of Educational Opportunity*, US Government, Washington.

Coleman, J. (1968). "The Concept of Equality of Educational Opportunity", *Harvard Educational Review*, vol. 38 (1).

Johnes, G. (1993). *The Economics of Education*, The MacMillan Press, London.

Kipp, S. (1998), *Demographic Trends: Their Impact on Future Undergraduate Enrolment and the Pell Program* Public dollars for Public Schools, OECD, Paris

Levin, H. (1983). *Educational Choice and the Pains of Democracy*, in James, T. and Levin, H. (eds). Public Dollars for Public Schools Temple U. Press, Philadelphia.

OECD (1998a). *Redifining Tertiary Education*, OECD, París.

OECD (1998b) *Educational Policy Analysis*, OECD, París

OECD (2000). *Education at a glance*, OECD, París.

UNESCO (1991). *The role of higher education in society: quality and pertinence*, The 2nd Unesco-Nongovermental Organizations Collective Consultation on Higher Education, 8-11 April 1991. Unesco, París, France. New Papers on Higher Education, 1.

Notes

[1] Data limitations require that the comparison of men and women be limited to university education.

[2] Diagram 4 gathers data from UNESCO on students enrolled in higher education. No data is available about graduates (as in diagrams 1 to 3, which use data from OECD).

[3] This is a study carried out in the USA by a team of researchers directed by the professor of sociology James Coleman, of the University of Chicago, as a result of the Civil Rights Law of 1964.

[4] Chapman (1998) and Kipp (1998) document similar inequalities in the access to higher education in Australia and the USA, respectively.

[5] In 1995, the European Union and in 1996, the OECD, published detailed reports that emphasize the lifelong learning policies.

[6] The incentives of individuals to invest in education and training in their youth make up one of the central predictions of the theory of human capital (Johnes, 1992).

Chapter Two

Access to higher education: the global agenda

Mary-Louise Kearney

Introduction

No discrimination can be accepted in granting access to higher education on grounds of race, gender, language or religion, or economic, cultural or social distinctions, or physical disabilities, (WCHE Declaration Article 3. a).

This pledge to equality of access and opportunity was given at the *World Conference on Higher Education, WCHE (Paris, October 1998)*. There, 5000 stakeholders made this commitment because of their vested interest in the benefits of tertiary teaching, training and research in today's knowledge society. Furthermore, the WCHE referred to the *'radically changing landscape of higher education'* which acknowledged the complex demands made upon this sector from many directions.

Access on merit, a main objectives of the WCHE, reaffirmed *Article 26.1 of the Universal Declaration of Human Rights*. This principle was accepted at the WCHE by many diverse groups who share a profound and common commitment to equality of opportunity. Certain questions are important:

- what is the reality of wider access to higher education?
- what are the consequences to date?
- what lessons have been learnt?
- what are the future paths for systems and institutions?

Since the 1998 WCHE, Member States and other stakeholders have moved swiftly to translate the vision into concrete action. However, much more needs to be done in terms of assuring access for all types of learners, including disadvantaged social groups and diversifying the provision available to serve this demand.

A global agenda for access to higher education implies:

- fostering a culture of access
- the realities of promoting access to specific fields, notably to lifelong learning, science and technical and vocational training
- the potential of wider access via NICT usage
- the impact on social development when higher education is widely accessible.

This analysis will draw on the ongoing efforts in relation to the applications of recent world conferences convened by UNESCO *(Lifelong Learning Hamburg 1997, Culture and Development Stockholm 1998, Higher Education Paris 1998, Technical and Vocational Education Seoul 1999, Science Budapest 1999 and – very importantly - the Education for All Assessment, Dakar 2000).* For all, access emerged as a central theme and a firm commitment.

Fostering a culture of access

Recognising cultural diversity

A culture of diversification in education rests on a prior recognition of the cultural diversity of society, *per se,* and of the need to deal with this reality in other policy areas.

The Intergovernmental Conference on Cultural Policies for Development (Stockholm 1998) described the cultural complexity inherent in the development dynamic of our era and the need to identify effective future strategies for dealing with this phenomenon in an increasingly multicultural world.

Our Cultural Diversity, the 1996 report of the World Commission on Culture and Development stressed that a global world will require a system of global ethics built on human rights and responsibilities, democracy and a strong civil society, the protection of minorities, commitment to peaceful conflict resolution and fair negotiation, and intergenerational equity.

Development must not lead to a loss of identity, of a sense of community or of personal meaning for certain segments of a given population. Rather, national development policies must promote the continuing creativity *in* and empowerment *of* all citizens, whatever their origin.

The response from education

These principles found their educational counterparts in the report of the International Commission on Education in the 21st Century entitled *Learning: the Treasure Within*. This suggested four basic pillars: learning to know; learning to do; learning to live together; learning to be.

As the foundation for education which would promote investment in the wide diversity constituted by human talent, special emphasis was given to 'learning to live together' as crucial for a world in which increased tolerance, understanding and mutual respect could deal with the challenges of growing interdependence and guard against conflict.

In tertiary education, the report further emphasised the shift towards a culture of diversification by indicating four major functions for institutions:

- the continued preparation of students for teaching and research
- the provision of training adapted to the needs of economic and social life
- meeting the needs of lifelong education in the widest sense
- engaging more actively in international co-operative action in favour of the developing world.

Tackling the numbers

Quantitative expansion and the provision of adequate resources are central issues for governments seeking to link education into more future-oriented social policy-making.

The *UNESCO Policy Paper for Change and Development in Higher Education* cited data to illustrate the process of growth and suggested that the figure of some 79 million students in 2000 might well rise to 100 million by 2025. Projected enrolments in the developing world are the most significant with increases of 25% - 33% expected. In a number of countries, enrolments continue to double (Turkey, Singapore, Chile) or triple (Guyana, Iran, Cyprus) - despite the persistence of the overall unequal opportunities for these populations in terms of their entry into post-secondary teaching and training. Elsewhere, the numbers clearly indicate the approach of mass tertiary education (Australia 72%, Canada 102%, Finland 67%, USA 81%).
(World Education Report , UNESCO 2000)

To cope with these factors, diversification of educational provision has been inevitable and has resulted in a greatly changed higher education sector within a relatively short space of time. This, in turn, has necessitated rethinking virtually every area of policy: resourcing, governance and management structures, academic careers and student services.

According to the 1998, OECD report *Redefining Tertiary Education*, continued expansion can be supported because:

• individuals recognise the value of quality education and training
• these are public 'goods' which help develop responsible and competent citizens able to contribute to social and economic progress
• the exclusion of significant areas of a population from the benefits of this level of education is potentially dangerous in terms of social cohesion. (OECD:102)

These advantages are echoed in the 2000 UNESCO/World Bank report entitled *Higher Education in Developing Countries : Peril and Promise* which holds that:

• the role of highly skilled human capital in development has become crucial, given the nature of society today, to help close the pernicious gap between wealth and poverty in a global world
• this type of human capital is the unique product of higher education.

Consequently, tertiary education - in its many diversified forms -is being reconsidered as an essential investment for these nations.

Diversification in knowledge, research and competences

A new mode of knowledge is emerging which is characterised by: production in the context of its application, transdisciplinarity, heterogeneity in the skills needed for its mastery, organizational diversity for its management, enhanced social accountability and a more broadly based system of quality control (Gibbons:6).

With regard to the tertiary sector, this new mode means that universities are **amongst** the actors in the knowledge business. But they must **re-configure** this to tackle pressing development problems and thus serve their surrounding societies. Achieving this in today's world requires an adequate degree of 'connectivity' which denotes the process of linkage to world-class research (usually via IT capacity) and the adaptation of this to local teaching, training and research which are undertaken by the academic community in close co-operation with the social counterparts concerned so that the relevance and application of these activities is both transparent and geared to results. In this way, higher education becomes a domain which is perceived as pertinent and practical by society at large and, at the same time, it can remain in close contact with international breakthroughs in knowledge creation.

Diversification also marks the types of research now undertaken. Various forces - global, social and economic - impact on research:

- basic research requires long term funding and capacities to ensure its sustainability
- contract research is often strongly oriented by the funding source and aims to produce strategic results inside a limited time-frame
- development-oriented research gives priority to linking enquiry to specific national problem-solving which often requires a transdisciplinary approach.
- quality research capacity - whether at national or institutional level - has become more precarious in all but the wealthiest contexts. Managing the diverse needs which require different types of investigation has become a necessity for all governments but constitutes a complex challenge.

Last but not least is the diversification in the competences required by students who will use their qualifications in a changing and volatile labour market. By now, it is well accepted that the mastery of knowledge *per se* is no longer enough - nor is it the expectation of the learner who considers that studies at the higher education level should prepare the person for a wide variety of functions.

Competences will vary according to the type of course taught - however, they were certainly easier to acquire when numbers were fewer and when student profiles were more homogeneous. Today, since both these factors are affected by the radical changes underway in the sector, the challenges faced by academic staff who must endeavour to provide skills-based teaching and learning experiences are manifold.

Diversifying the resource base

Today, the tertiary sector faces high societal expectations and specific economic requirements. The WCHE Commission on Management and Financing considered that the challenge is threefold:

- to diversify and increase the resource base
- to achieve further economies and greater effectiveness by more creative use of all types of resources
- to gain a wider understanding and acceptance of the value of investing in the sector within the community itself.

Wider access must be funded and so diversifying the resource base is a task for systems and institutions alike.

Promoting access to specific fields

The availability of lifelong learning

The 5th International Conference on Adult Education (CONFITEA V, Hamburg 1997) discussed the broad and complex spectrum of adult education under ten major categories:

- adult learning and democracy
- improving the conditions and quality of such learning
- ensuring the universal right to literacy and basic education
- gender equality
- the changing world of work
- its links to the environment, health and population
- its relations with culture, the media and the NITs
- adult education for all: the rights of different groups
- the economics of adult learning systems
- enhancing international co-operation in this field.

Access to science and technology

Here, access is pertinent in a variety of ways:

- for development, science has become 'a currency in the hierarchy of nations' (Article 2.1, Para. 15). It is essential that the scientific priorities of each country be satisfied so as to reduce the gap between the haves and have-nots in this area;
- for science education, renewal, expansion and diversification were identified as urgent to ensure that all countries can have a stake in the society of the future (Article 2.4. Para 22);
- regarding higher science education and research, their links must be reinforced to produce the critical mass of scientists needed in every country for its genuine development (Article

2.4. Para 23); allied to this are the current trends affecting university research in areas such as funding, personnel, interface with industry, and its pre-eminence in the knowledge complex. As a result, many of the givens of the past have been superseded by new factors emanating from the new global order which require major adaptation on the part of universities themselves;

- wider participation in the scientific enterprise for all groups, including women, is a human right and due account must be taken of the increasingly diverse actors now entering scientific areas (Article 3.3. para.33).

The potential of technical and vocational education

The 2nd International Congress on Technical and Vocational Education (TVET) (Seoul 1999) stressed:

- the importance of the economics of TVET for countries which seek to increase their investment in development-relevant education and training;
- the complexity surrounding the social status of TVET which is inextricably linked to how a given community values work in both intellectual and practical terms;
- the growing regional and international dimensions of TVET in globalized economies which take account of factors such as the changing structure of world trade, labour mobility, common markets, commodity standards and the influence of multinationals.

Education for all assessment (Dakar 2000)

Factors which have caused the EFA mission to evolve are:

- growth in systemic knowledge and understanding of the impact of the wider environment on education
- a succession of world conferences on global issues with direct educational implications
- heightened public awareness of global interdependence and imbalances.

Access via NICT

Facilitated access

That technology has opened horizons is not in doubt. Examples abound: the Open University of the United Kingdom now organizes its graduate ceremony online, Phoenix University in Arizona, USA, enrols over 60,000 students, mostly mid-career adults who appreciate its practical curriculum; networks of universities e.g. Universitas 21, the U.Next.Com (a consortium of highly regarded American Business Schools), the British E-University are already offering degree courses via IT.

Educational institutions have clearly been able to emulate other global networks which can shrink time and space to meet demand. In many instances, their management and teaching structures have successfully responded to demand. And, in the developing world, the awareness to compete on the global market via virtual learning facilities has been heightened. Open universities are well established in Thailand, Tanzania and Latin America. The African Virtual University, an experimental project of the World Bank, is now very close to operating as an independent entity to serve the needs of the region. Great interest is manifested from the Arab region where large and young populations require rapid entry to post-secondary education and training.

Issues to be addressed

Technology statistics attest to the gravity of unequal access:
- 80% of the world's population lack access to telecommunications
- by 2010, 40% of all new jobs will be technology-based - yet the purchase of a computer represents several years of average wages in the least developed countries
- certain LDCs (e.g. Haiti, Sierra Leone, Bangladesh) have less than 1 telephone line per 100 persons
- in the USA, 1 in 3 people has INTERNET; in South Asia, 1 in 10,000 persons is online
- Thailand has more cellular phones than the whole of Africa.
(Source: HDR 1999)

Clearly, more research is required to assess the true quality of the new technological paradigm in education, and its ability to respond satisfactorily to current issues of concern for higher education such as regional diversity, co-development, scientific excellence, intellectual property, the compatibility of teaching materials and quality assurance.

Conclusion: future concerns

'Our challenge is to move beyond rhetoric and recognize that we live in a time of astonishing possibility..... solutions to problems which seemed insurmountable just a few years ago are now within reach,' (Wolfensohn IHT 28 January 2000).

In the future, tertiary education must demonstrate clear commitment to three major objectives:

- promoting all citizens' participation in development
- reinforcing the Learning Society
- ensuring the quality and relevance of this new order.

Citizens' participation in development

In many areas exclusion from advanced education and training is preventing poverty alleviation and - instead - maintaining exclusion from equitable social development. Further reform and diversification seem inevitable to arrive at true citizen participation - in order to ensure that the principle of access for all to this sector is translated into reality.

Reinforcing the Learning Society

Participation requires access to robust learning organisations: i.e. companies, schools, universities, cities and any country or group committed to progress through learning. Such organizations:

- invest in their own future
- create opportunities for all
- share their future vision with interested partners who are invited to contribute to its realization
- integrate work and learning
- mobilise human talent
- empower all people
- offer many ways to learn
- respond proactively to the wider needs of society
- learn and relearn how to maintain energy and innovation.

Ensuring the quality and relevance of the new order

Quality has been defined as fitness for purpose, which recognises the diversity of higher education missions and provision. Relevance requires tertiary education to play a varied and complex role in a rapidly changing social environment. Access to higher education must be situated in this complex environment. Above all, education and training of human capital remains the primary goal because this has emerged as the most valuable resource of all nations as they face the realities of the Knowledge Society.

Evaluation procedures

One of the major challenges facing systems and institutions is finding and applying reliable ways of measuring their progress towards the goal of wider access for more diverse groups of learners, including those from traditionally disadvantaged groups. This is where the proof of good intentions can be put to the test in a climate of social change where knowledge and know-how are the keys to national and personal advancement to a much greater extent than ever before.

Articles 1 and 2 of the Framework for Priority Action for Change and Development in Higher Education emphasize action to be taken by national decision-makers to reach the goal of wider access. However, Member States and their responsible bodies are dealing with this complex task in difficult conditions where the increased demand for post-secondary education is set against a background of sparse financial and human resources.

Practical indicators are therefore needed to help these authorities assess their progress towards their commitment to wider admission. A study commissioned by UNESCO has listed available indicators from sources such as the UNESCO Statistical Yearbook and the OECD's Education at a Glance. These permit countries to measure their results in key areas such as the number of students per 100,000 inhabitants, gender balance, distribution per discipline, the choice of studies made by older learners, current expenditure on tertiary level education and on research and development, learner profiles and their backgrounds, and numbers of teachers. As a complementary element, indicators which do not exist and thus should be collected are also listed. Gaps to be filled include fuller details on the socio-economic, cultural and ethnic profiles of learners, the availability of bridging courses to encourage wider access, the status of 'e-learning' as a means of broadening admission, the participation of individual countries in legal instruments which foster access (such as conventions on academic mobility), and the countrywide mechanisms to facilitate the involvement of both academics and the industrial sector in the national research agenda (Fielden and Abercromby: 25-30).

Though designed as a first and experimental step, this study will lead to other more detailed analyses of access and the complex aspects presented by the policy. Moreover, the study highlighted the imperative for all countries, notably those in the developing world, to strengthen their statistical capacities in order to arrive at reliable evaluation of their progress and of their performance compared with that of their counterparts elsewhere. Without this capacity, data on access cannot be considered to be fully reliable.

References

Altbach, Philip (1998) *Knowledge, the University and Development*. JAI Press, London.

Altbach, Philip (Ed.) (1999) *Private Higher Education and Development in the 21st Century*. Greenwood Publishing, Boston College.

Burgess, Robert L. (Ed.) (1998) *Beyond the First Degree*. London, SRHE.

Clark, Burton (1998) *Creating Entrepreneurial Universities*. Pergamon, U. K.

Fielden, John and Abercromm Karen by 2000. UNESCO Higher Education Indicators Study: *Accountability and International Co-operation in the Renewal of Higher Education*. Paris, UNESCO.

Gibbons, Michael (1998) *Higher Education Relevance for the 21st Century*. World Bank, Washington.

Giddens, Anthony (1999) *The Third Way*. London, Polity Press.

HoldenRonning, Anne and Kearney, Mary-Louise (Eds.)(1998) *Graduate Profiles in a Changing Society*. (UNESCO/IOHE)

OECD (1998) *Redefining Tertiary Education*. Paris.

Scott, Peter (Ed.) (1999) *The Globalization of Higher Education*. London, SRHE.

UNDP (1999) The Human Development Report. New York.

UNESCO (1996) *Learning: The Treasure Within*. Report on Education for the XXI Century. Paris,

UNESCO (1995) Policy Paper for Change and Development in Higher Education. Paris.

UNESCO (2000) The World Education Report. Paris.

UNESCO (1998) World Declaration and Priority Framework for Action. World Conference on Higher Education. Paris.

World Bank/UNESCO (2000) *Higher Education in Developing Countries: Peril and Promise*. Report of the Independent World Bank/UNESCO Task Force. Washington.

Chapter Three

Supporting widening participation:
UCAS – forecasting and planning who applies to study what and where

Gaie Davidson-Burnet and Liz Peters

Introduction

A key educational policy of the current United Kingdom (UK) Government is to encourage students from those groups that have previously been under-represented on higher education courses to apply and, where able, be accepted by universities and colleges onto tertiary level programmes of study. Both Further and Higher Education Funding Councils are supporting institutions by providing funding for research projects into this area[1]. Sector bodies, such as the Universities and Colleges Admissions Service (UCAS), are also actively engaged in developing services that can assist institutions in identifying those groups of students who are under-represented within their establishment and supporting them in their efforts to widen access to their programmes of study.

This chapter first outlines the tripartite Forecasting & Planning Service, which the Department of Research & Statistics at UCAS has designed to support planning and widening access initiatives in universities and colleges. Second, with reference to a survey of universities and colleges undertaken in 1999/2000, it notes the hurdles that institutions face when they try to employ the tripartite services, and considers which internal practices they may need to review and the additional measures UCAS might take to support them.

The Role of UCAS

UCAS was established in 1993 from the merger of the Universities Central Council on Admissions (UCCA), the Polytechnics Central Admissions System (PCAS) and the Standing Conference on University Entrance (SCUE). In its first year, 179 institutions offered places to approximately 403,000 potential students applying through UCAS on just under 40,000 full-time undergraduate courses. This academic year it is anticipated that almost half a million potential students will apply to over 45,000 courses in 336 UCAS member institutions. This increase in the number of institutions to which potential students could apply and courses from which they might select, together with the increasing numbers of people actually applying through UCAS might indicate that widening access is already occurring. Certainly the higher education sector is expanding, and more students are being admitted to study in higher education institutions year on year[2]. However, universities and colleges need to know whether they are merely admitting more of the same type of student as had applied and been accepted previously, or actually encouraging people from under- represented groups to apply and gain entrance.

UCAS holds data collected from the applications forms that all potential full-time undergraduate students complete at the start of the admissions cycle. It covers the demographic characteristics of applicants to higher education courses provided by universities and colleges in England, Wales, Scotland and Northern Ireland, those who are offered places, and those who are finally accepted to study. Data includes applicants' age, gender, social class, ethnicity and, where applicable, their disability, and the courses and institutions to which they applied. Additionally, data is held on applicants' entry qualifications, which is received directly from the examination and assessment boards in the summer before applicants hope to enter their chosen courses, and the last educational establishment they attended. Data is held from 1994 to the current cycle and is unique in that it provides an insight not only into the characteristics of those people who are accepted onto full-time undergraduate courses, but also on those who would have liked to have been accepted, but were not. It is this area of information provision that UCAS is uniquely positioned to support institutions in their efforts to widen participation.

Four levels of data are made available to UCAS member institutions, both during and after the admissions cycle. First, universities and colleges receive management statistics regarding their applicants and the courses and institutions to which they have applied, and aggregate data for the sector as a whole and for the previous year[3]. Second, comparative data is available for six or more clusters of institutions within national or regional boundaries, or with similar profiles. Third, increasingly, data is provided which addresses the slightly differing requirements of English, Scottish, Welsh and Northern Irish institutions, their associated funding councils and national Parliaments and Assemblies. Finally, UCAS data is being enhanced by the addition of other data sources, such as information on schools and colleges, the economic performance of local regions, the profiles of inhabitants in specified geographic locations and their distance from institutions.

The Forecasting & Planning Service

The UCAS Forecasting & Planning Service presents members with a tripartite service composed of three complementary elements: the Institutional Planning Service (IPS), the Applicant Postcode Tracking Service (APTS) and the Forecasting Service (FS). The IPS uses *past* data, to enable institutions to identify trends within the sector and to benchmark themselves against institutions they consider similar to themselves. The APTS allows institutions to monitor their applicants to the courses they offer during the *current* live cycle on safe areas of the UCAS website. The FS permits institutions to forecast the numbers and profiles of people who are likely to apply to their university or college in the *future* and accept their offer of a place. Together, these three services help institutions to explore the nature of their recruitment patterns and to target groups of applicants and potential applicants in line with their widening participation policies.

1 The Institutional Planning Service (IPS)

At the close of each admissions cycle (31 October), UK sector data is prepared and placed in seven Excel datasets on the UCAS website at[4] The datasets[5] include:
- Subject Dataset
- Institution/ Subject Group/ Domicile Dataset
- Institution/ Age Dataset
- Region/ Domicile Dataset
- Qualifications/ Subject Dataset
- Qualifications/ Educational Establishment/ Ethnicity Dataset
- Ethnicity/ Social Class Dataset

Comparison of the information presented within these datasets year on year from 1996 illustrates the application and acceptance trends within the higher education sector as a whole. In order that institutions may obtain a clearer picture of how they are performing relative to other institutions, the IPS also offers institutional datasets that contain a selection of an institution's own applicant data and that of six or more others institutions aggregated data. These are available in five key areas[6]: Institutional Planning Service (IPS), Applicant: Applications, Clearing, Competitor, Regional, and Subject[7].

2 The Applicant Postcode Tracking Service (APTS)

The Applicant Postcode Tracking Service (APTS) is a web-based service offered to each UCAS member institution. At the start of each application cycle, university and college staff can access, by a password, secure parts of the UCAS website and monitor each individual applicant to the various courses they offer. Applicants are located on maps by their postcodes, and users can interrogate the system at postcode area (GL), postcode district (GL54) or postcode sector level (GL54 5).

To each individual applicant's postcode address is attached a geo-demographic profile called a lifestyle group[8], designed and supplied by the company Experian[9]. The geo-demographic instrument provides a fine level of detail down to 15 houses, and provides institutions with an overview of those geographical areas from which potential students are either over- or under-applying[10]. Institutions may interrogate applications from pupils attending various schools and colleges throughout the UK, the courses they apply to, their lifestyle group, age, gender, and applicant status[11]. Data is available for the current and previous year, and includes UK benchmarks, which enable institutions to compare the MOSAIC profile of their applicants to different subjects and establish whether their potential cohorts reflect or deviate from trends within the sector. It is hoped that institutions will use this service to monitor whether their widening participation initiatives are encouraging people from under-represented areas to apply in greater numbers than previously[12].

3 The Forecasting Service (FS)

The Forecasting Service (FS) is a new service currently designed to help institutions in their selection process. Datasets are based around two themes: catchment areas and conversion rates. Each dataset offers five years of data (1996-2000) relating to universities' and colleges' own applicants, what subjects they applied to and where they were eventually accepted. The data enables institutions to explore changes in the social class, ethnic origin and MOSAIC profiles of their applicants and whether the distance they are prepared to travel has altered over time. It is hoped that universities and colleges will use the data to predict whether there are catchment areas and schools that should be targeted to increase representation of people from under-represented areas, and to establish which characteristics influence the acceptability of applicants.

Data is enhanced with the addition of applicants' MOSAIC profile, the distance from their home or boarding school to the institutions to which they are applying, and the performance of the school and college they are either currently attending or had previously attended[13].

4 Interactive on line Statistical Enquiry Service

To support the tripartite service, UCAS also offers visitors to its website an interactive on-line Statistical Enquiry Service, which enables users to create customised information on the web. Data for the UK may be interrogated for the years 1996 to 2000 inclusive and variables for the columns and rows are available in pull-down menus with a full glossary available. As users select the contents of the tables they are building, a box in the top right hand of the screen shows what has been chosen: the year of entry, variables included in the rows and columns, and the sum total.

Evaluating the service

Results of a survey of UCAS member institutions

From August 1999 until March 2000, three members of the Department of Research & Statistics visited a representative sample of UCAS member institutions to evaluate the design and piloting of the tripartite Forecasting & Planning Service[14]. Fifty member institutions and sector organisations were selected for visits. They were chosen to represent universities and colleges throughout the regions of England, Northern Ireland, Scotland and Wales of varying sizes, ages, campus arrangements and subject provision. Since the internal structure of universities and colleges differs considerably in the UK, invitations were sent to a wide selection of offices where it was considered staff might use the tripartite service. Staff in the admissions, marketing, planning, policy-making, school and college liaison, and widening participation offices attended a two-hour presentation and fed back their comments both during the sessions and subsequently in paper and electronic form.

Evaluation of the Institutional Planning Service (IPS)

Staff in most institutions were aware of the Institutional Planning Service (87%), but within institutions the knowledge of how the IPS could be used varied enormously. A considerable number of planning staff (92%), who were familiar with Excel spreadsheets, used the pivot tables to manipulate the data. Quite a good number of marketing staff could also use spreadsheets, but many of them were not aware that the IPS was provided to institutions (less than 50%). Among admissions staff, awareness of the IPS was patchy and thirty per cent

(30%) expressed considerable fear of the technical expertise that is required to optimally use the spreadsheets. Policy staff (Pro-Vice-Chancellors, registrars, and members of the Vice-Chancellor's office) expressed considerable enthusiasm for the IPS (82%), usually in the context of the overall developments (including the two pilot services). Unfortunately, those staff who were engaged directly in widening access programmes were often unaware of the service.

Of the three elements of the IPS, the 15 December 1999 Management Statistics datasets were greeted with the greatest enthusiasm. The Excel spreadsheet contains four variables:
1. all the institutions applied to by an institutions applicants
2. the subjects groups applied to
3. the subject lines applied to
4. the number of applications received at 15 December.

Demonstration of the statistics showed staff how they could rank order the number of applications made to both subject groups and subject lines at their institution and those also applied to by their applicants. The different rank ordering between institutions when subject groups were changed appeared to be a novel finding to many staff, and particularly engaged policy-makers.

Many institutional staff knew that the annual datasets were available from the UCAS website each December following entry cycle. Planning and marketing officers expressed reasonable familiarity with the datasets, but admissions staff stated that they had little time to develop the expertise required for adequate data manipulation. Widening access staff were often unaware of the datasets.

Evaluation of the Applicant Postcode Tracking Service (APTS)

The majority of interviewees were delighted to view the information that is usually received on separate application forms on web-based maps of the UK (78%). Schools and colleges liaison officers showed particular interest in the different distribution of applicants across the UK by various subject groups. In those institutions where selection is the focus of admissions, the ability of the APTS to highlight those parts of the country from which no applications had been received was welcomed. The ability of the service to zoom in and identify the schools in those areas was seen as an excellent opportunity to target schools in an effort to widen participation (92%). Others found the different institutional MOSAIC distributions per subject group, benchmarked against national distributions, was useful for estimating the degree to which institutions deviated from aggregate figures (61%). The ability of the service to list all candidates from a school applying to a variety of courses was thought potentially useful to expand the range of courses applied to by pupils, particularly those that did not recruit well. Most widening access staff had not been given the password to access the UCAS website and use this service.

Evaluation of the Forecasting Service (FS)

Reaction to the Forecasting Service ranged from rapturous responses '*This is precisely what UCAS should be doing*' to the dismissive '*But I know all that already*'. As a large part of the presentation focused on the conceptual use of data and analysis rather than the practical use of a service, interest within institutions tended to come from those with some level of technical and/or statistical expertise. Fifty per cent (50%) of institutions welcomed the analysis in terms of predicting accepted applicants and this figure rose to 78% when longer-term forecasts, which included time-series analysis were discussed. Sixty per cent (60%) of institutions considered that the service would enhance their understanding of the profile of their likely accepted applicants and enable them to gain some indication of subjects where recruitment might not be on target or where widening access might be a concern.

Evaluation of the on line interactive Statistical Enquiry Service

Staff considered this enquiry service a useful adjunct to the more sophisticated IPS service. Many were surprised at the ease and speed with which tables were constructed, although a number expressed concern that people unfamiliar with UCAS terminology might mistake applicants for applications or confuse applications to degree and sub degree courses.

Lessons from the evaluation

Issues for Universities and Colleges

The investigation highlighted the dispersed nature of many tasks within institutions that use UCAS data. In some institutions there was a close sharing of knowledge and data between different areas of responsibility; in others there was not. Where roles and responsibilities were known and shared, there tended to be a greater awareness of what data institutions received from UCAS and how it might be used. In the oldest institutions included in this survey, data was passed to both administrative and academic staff for analysis; this did not occur in universities and colleges established more recently[15]. Where there was not a high level of technical skill or sufficient personnel to hone the abilities required for data manipulation, UCAS data was not used to its full capacity.

In general, where there were clear links between the policy-makers within an institution and those staff technically able to handle data, the best use of UCAS data was made. However, in almost all institutions, the pressure of work and the changing demands of external parties meant that insufficient time was committed to exploring the possibilities that the data offers. In some institutions, this is compounded by older software, which hinders the exploration of the new services involving web- based services and spreadsheet manipulation.

A number of staff commented that the provision of these services by an organisation known to administer admissions meant that universities and colleges might have to consider their internal structures and who could access such information. At present, UCAS services must be channelled through the UCAS correspondent; a post usually held by a person who is located in an institution's registry. People assigned the task of widening access may be part of an administrative, academic or academic-related structure. In some institutions, a pro-vice chancellor who oversees academic planning may also oversee a widening access team, in others widening access staff may be placed in each faculty or school and co-ordinated from a central administrative hub, in yet others, widening access may be part of an outreach section. The variation within institutions of where the responsibility for widening access is located makes it difficult for an external agency to identify where information about a service should be directed. Within institutions, knowledge of who could benefit from awareness of such services is problematic. Titles do not necessarily convey the tasks associated with the role. Communications channels are not necessarily established between those who receive information about services and those who might best benefit from using them. Finally, the level of technical skill required effectively to deploy all three services is rarely found outside planning and marketing offices.

In those universities and colleges where the Forecasting & Planning Services are being used to support widening access projects, channels of communication permit easy access to information and data, staff are technically proficient, and institutions are prepared to share their passwords to the UCAS website with collaborating organisations[16]. In many institutions, however, barriers regarding the ownership of data, access to information, and collaboration between administrative and academic staff are hindering the use of the services to widen access. These issues, as well as technical proficiency, liaison between policy-makers and practitioners, and institutional mission raise matters which both institutions and UCAS need to address.

Issues for UCAS

Although institutional staff welcomed the initiatives being taken by UCAS to make data more available for widening access, planning, marketing, schools and colleges liaison as well as for the process of admissions, concern was expressed that insufficient promotion of the services or training required to access them was available. UCAS was asked to consider how to promote to institutions and other bodies those services that can be offered by using admissions data as well as offering an admissions service. This will necessitate identifying those products and services that should be included within the capitation fee, which member institutions annually pay, and those that may be offered additional to the fee. The Forecasting & Planning Service was asked to consider offering a training service, which would train institutional staff to use the tripartite service effectively. It was also asked to consider offering an analytical service for those institutions that would prefer UCAS to undertake an analysis of data for them. Fundamental to the development of any new services, however, UCAS was asked to promote these services to all staff in institutions who might benefit from using them.

Conclusions: how the Forecasting & Planning Services can help universities and colleges widen participation

The challenges which UCAS, universities and colleges face as they collaborate to widen access to under-represented groups are several. Institutions need to investigate the established ways in which particular roles and responsibilities are allocated within their organisations and see whether there may be better ways of sharing information that has traditionally been the preserve of one area. In particular, where new or contract staff are engaged upon widening participation projects, it could be helpful if a list of information and data sources could be made available to them at the start of the project. Such information could be provided by the funding bodies, reside on websites frequently accessed by researchers (e.g. SRHE), or disseminated by sector organisations.

UCAS needs to explore the ways in which other services may be developed using the data it holds which may additionally serve the interests of its member institutions. In particular, it is apparent that a service that could support staff in understanding the data that is available in the sector, how to access it and how to use it optimally would be appreciated. More pressing is the issue that UCAS currently faces of having only one point of contact in its member institutions: the UCAS correspondent. It is not adequate to make data available to institutions through a contact point that few researchers know about or, conversely, expect a person charged with admissions duties to be aware of all the academic, academic-related and administrative initiatives to widen access. If sector organisations are to support widening participation initiatives, they must incorporate these aims into their corporate plans and ensure that they adopt adequate strategies to make them a success.

Notes

[1] The Further Education Funding Council is to be replaced by the Learning Skills Council in April 2001. England, Wales and Scotland each have there own funding council, Northern Ireland is administered by the Higher Education Funding Council for England.

[2] In 1994, 270,000 applicants were accepted to full-time undergraduate courses offered by UCAS member institutions compared with 330,000 in 1999, 'Statistical Bulletin on Widening Participation', Edition 2000, UCAS.

[3] Data is confidential to institutions and only divulged to third parties with the express permission of an institution's chief officer.

[4] All UCAS datasets are prepared as Excel 5 since this version is standard amongst most member institutions. Datasets are limited to 16,000 rows. Details of the variables included in each of the datasets are listed on the UCAS website at www.ucas.com/figures/fps/index.html under 'Institutional Planning Service'.

[5] Variables included in each annual dataset have been selected to permit the broadest coverage of data in the most efficient manner.

[6] Data is aggregated to ensure that information about a single institution or applicant remains confidential. Where institutions agree to share data and formally notify UCAS, named institutional information is available. All Medical Schools in the UK have agreed to share and release named data in the interests of widening access and promoting greater transparency within the admissions process. Data regarding the characteristics of applicants to Medical Schools is available on the UCAS website and may also be accessed from the Council of Heads of Medical Schools website at www.chms.ac.uk.

[7] Details of the contents of each of the datasets is available from the UCAS website at the above address under 'Institutional Planning Service'.

[8] MOSAIC is a geo-demographic tool used to classify residential postcode areas into distinct neighbourhood types based on statistical information about people who live in them. It uses

a combination of census, electoral role, housing and financial data to classify households into 12 groups.

[9] Definitions of each of the twelve MOSAIC categories are available on the APTS.

[10] UCAS does not supply information to institutions concerning an individual applicant's social class or ethnicity until the close of the cycle. Institutions requested the adoption of this procedure to ensure compliance with their statutes.

[11] Applicant status changes throughout the application cycle as individual applicants are made offers (conditional or unconditional) by universities and colleges, whether they accept or reject two of these offers as firm or insurance, and, when their results are published, whether they have met their conditions or not.

[12] MOSAICs are not substitutes for social class, as assigned by parental or highest household earner's occupation, but are broad indicators of lifestyles associated within geographical neighbourhoods

[13] Performance is measured in terms of the percentage of accepted applicants from a school in the past.

[14] The sample included the: University of Aberdeen, Anglia Polytechnic University, University if Wales Bangor, University of Bath, Bath Spa University College, University of Birmingham, Bournemouth University, University if Bradford, University of the West of England (Bristol), University of Cambridge, University of Wales Institute Cardiff, University of Central Lancashire, Cheltenham and Gloucester College of Higher Education, Chester (A College of the University of Liverpool), Coventry University, Dartington College of Arts, Edge Hill College of Higher Education, University of Edinburgh, University of Exeter, Glasgow Caledonian University, Gloucestershire College of Arts and Technology, Heriot-Watt University (Edinburgh), Imperial College of Science, Technology and Medicine, University of Kent at Canterbury, University of Lancaster, Liverpool Hope University, London Guildhall University, London School of Economics and Political Science, Napier University, University of Oxford, Oxford Brookes University, Plymouth University, the Queen's University of Belfast, Robert Gordon University, Sheffield Hallam University, St Martin's College Lancaster, Ambleside, Carlisle, College of St Mark and St John, University of Strathclyde, Sunderland University, University of Sussex, University of Wales Swansea, University of Teeside, University of Ulster, Westminster University, University College Worcester. Department of Higher & Further Education and Training (Northern Ireland), Higher Education Funding Council for England, Higher Education Funding Council for Wales, Scottish Higher Education

Funding Council, Scottish Executive Office, and the Welsh Assembly

[15] Report of the Vice-Chancellor' Working Party on Access', University of Oxford (May 1999)

[16] 'Using Applicant Tracking Systems and Performance Indicators to Design, Target and Monitor Strategies Aimed at Widening Participation', Michael Hill, Kingston University, UK. EAN Annual Convention, Santiago 3-6 September 2000, Session 5.1

Chapter Four

'Mind the quality and feel the width' - a framework for evaluating widening participation strategies in post-compulsory education

Jan Smith

Introduction

'Evaluation' in this chapter is used in a very broad sense to mean any strategy for judging progress. It includes the use of national performance indicators and the evaluation of institutional strategies at the 'macro' level, to evaluation of small-scale projects at the 'micro' level. As there is some overlap in methodology and purpose between research and evaluation, the role of research is addressed later in this chapter.

Evaluation of widening participation initiatives at national level has tended to focus on quantitative data, ('number crunching') and to be about accountability, ('proving the case'), while small-scale evaluations are more likely to include qualitative data and to focus on what can be learned ('improving'). The author takes the view that while all these approaches have made a contribution to raising the profile of or improving practice in widening participation, the outcomes of evaluation have made little impact on the wider audience which this hitherto 'Cinderella' area of practice deserves.

This chapter attempts to look at some of the reasons why this is the case and to proposes a framework for a more holistic approach. It begins by looking at 'macro' level evaluation, the level which concerns institutions and national policy-makers and moves on to the 'micro' level which is more the concern of programme managers and researchers.

Over the last four years, government funding in the UK has supported a variety of projects aimed at widening participation, and the funding has come with the requirement that the project will be evaluated. Individual projects have varied considerably in their purpose and scope, and therefore the approach to evaluation has also varied. As universities in England are now required to produce statements outlining their strategies for widening participation, with targets and measurable outcomes, there should now be an institutional dimension to the evaluation of strategies. There is therefore an appropriate moment to review the options for evaluation and consider how to maximise the influence of reports. There are opportunities in this institutional context to raise the profile of widening participation, bring issues of concern to the attention of senior managers and others, as well as to develop practice.

The 'macro' level

Approaches to measuring and assuring quality ('macro' versions of evaluation) have mushroomed in education sectors across the developed world over the last decade, strongly influenced by industrial models. The higher education sector has not escaped this influence, but until recently, there has been a weak match between the concerns of those working in the field of widening participation, and performance measurement at this 'macro' level.

The use of performance indicators in education, which proliferate at the 'macro' level, have been criticised as selective, imprecise, reductionist, and in the context of league tables, divisive. There are in addition some particular difficulties associated with their application to widening participation:

* The work is often of a developmental and experimental nature, dealing with the new rather than the norm. It is difficult therefore to tie success exclusively to one or two indicators.

* Many activities are a long-term investment and the application of short-term measures may be inappropriate. For example, outreach activities in schools often begin with fourteen year-old (Year 9) students, with a higher education participation target that cannot be measured until the end of year 13.

* Much of the work is focused on qualitative and attitudinal change. Strategies to raise aspirations and awareness of higher education (HE) are examples. It may be easier therefore to attempt to evaluate this and to neglect key indicators such as actual participation in HE.

- There are particular problems in categorising students. For example, 'non-standard entry', a category used in the collection of UK HE statistics at institutional level[1], covers a wide range of groups of students whose backgrounds are likely to vary considerably. Mature students who have come through a customised access course route and nineteen-year-olds entering HE with a pre-vocational qualification are lumped together for statistical purposes.

- Progress on social inclusion is especially difficult to tie to one indicator. Proxy indicators such as fee waiver, neighbourhood groups, postcodes or parental occupation are all problematic for various reasons, and do not take account of cultural or attitudinal differences.

There is a danger in avoiding the use of performance indicators, however, as there is a need to demonstrate progress in this area of work through criteria which are clear, and perceived to be objective. In terms of social inclusion, there is ample evidence, most of which is quantitative, to show how little progress has been made in widening participation in HE to disadvantaged groups. In spite of the so called 'massification' of HE and the many initiatives to include under-represented groups, the socio-economic profile of the HE student population in the UK remains stubbornly biased towards middle and upper class and upper-middle class groups despite the expansion of HE (Dearing, 1997).

Now that access and social inclusion are more central to UK government policy concerns, there are signs that the collection and use of data will be more helpful in identifying progress. New indicators for access developed by the funding councils in England, Northern Ireland, Scotland and Wales (HEFCE, 1999) are based on the following:

- the proportion of students who previously attended a state school or college
- those whose parents' occupation is classed as skilled manual, semi-skilled or unskilled
- those whose home is in a low participation area, identified by post-code.

As these indicators have been developed in consultation with higher education institutions, the funding councils are aware of some of the concerns over their application. The report giving the first comprehensive set of data using these indicators (HEFCE, ibid) advises caution over how the data is used. It warns against comparing dissimilar institutions, stresses the importance of recognising different institutional missions, and sets the figures in the context of benchmarks for institutions with a similar profile.

While this focus on measuring progress on social inclusion is welcome, large-scale quantitative approaches can mask important issues, two of which are highlighted here. They relate to the approach currently used in the UK, but could apply to 'macro' level use of performance indicators anywhere.

The first concerns the use of 'benchmarking', increasingly used as a means of 'notching up' performance in education. In the UK model, the application of this to widening participation actually conceals the dismal performance of many universities. The benchmarks are based on the entry profile of similar groups of institutions, and as there is a strong correlation between this and the socio-economic profile of the students, the baseline for comparison is very different. Some institutions (mainly the 'old' universities) take a much higher proportion of upper middle-class students than others, and they are compared with those who also have a poor track record in terms of social inclusion. This, it can be argued, goes beyond 'taking account of institutional differences' and simply 'normalises' elitism.

A further problem is the way the level of aggregation conceals pattern of non-participation by particular groups. While overall participation by gender, ethnicity and disability has improved, Roper, Ross and Thomson (2000) point to the major gender imbalance in certain curriculum areas such as engineering and science, to the under-representation of Bangladeshi females and Afro-Caribbean males in UK universities as a whole, and to the concentration of ethnic minority groups in certain universities. If these imbalances are considered a problem and a reflection of inequalities in the education system, then a means of measuring progress which ignores these disparities is clearly flawed.

To address these two weaknesses in the methodology and to include lifelong learning in the indicators of social inclusion, Roper *et al* (ibid) propose three alternative measures: [2]

1. *'Added' social inclusion*: that is, how far each institution in each subject band contributes to the inclusion of all socially excluded groups and all ethnic groups in a gender neutral manner. Performance indicators would be weighted so that recruitment of, for example, male students to teaching was recognised as redressing an imbalance.

2. *Added economic value of institutions*; this would measure the added economic value of a degree for a given university. It would be arrived at by comparing the average earnings of a graduate from a particular institution with the earnings of a similar person of the same age with the same entry qualifications but with no degree.

3. Lifelong learning as measured by:

i.   Age on admission index of full and part-time students to show how good institutions are at recruiting through life post-school

ii. Measure of how far institutions are recognising and valuing post-school qualifications

iii. Index of proportion of part-time students to show how much an institution is allowing students to study concurrently with 'life' outside.

The authors propose linking this approach to the funding mechanism so that institutions are directly rewarded for their contribution to social inclusion as defined by these indicators. While this is an interesting approach, it does not take account of the different subject mix across institutions, or the relative difficulty of achieving change in some subject areas (in medicine, for example).

There are other more general limitations to 'macro' accountability models, with their reliance on performance indicators. First, a funding carrot (or stick) is needed to pull into line those who do not share the values implicit in the methodology. Second, it can only describe and not explain, 'prove' but not 'improve'. Third, there is the obvious risk of missing important but unexpected qualitative outcomes when using only pre-determined measures. Given all these problems, it is easy to dismiss macro level and quantitative methods as unhelpful and irrelevant. On the other hand, to ignore it is effectively to undermine the importance of evaluating progress in widening participation.

'Micro' level

While finding effective and diverse ways to assess the impact of institutional strategies requires more than large-scale number crunching, the diversity has proved easier to achieve than the effectiveness. At the 'micro' level of a small-scale project, for example, the duration of the project may make effective evaluation difficult to plan and deliver. The use of performance indicators in general, and quantitative data in particular, may be resisted, so that the data generated (through, for example, a collection of case studies) remains anecdotal and difficult to link to any general principles of effective practice.

The author's recent experience of researching practice through a regional widening participation project illustrates this[3]. The purpose of the research was to identify effective strategies for widening participation to higher education. It included the analysis of existing evaluation reports of a variety of small-scale initiatives and projects, such as school visits to a university, 'taster' days and courses for mature students, a black mentoring scheme, and a 'take your daughters to work' day.

Analysis showed that there was little consistency between the approaches used, even where the evaluations came from the same institution, and limited use of specific performance indicators. Although many of the activities and projects were targeted at particular populations, it was sometimes impossible to show how successful this targeting had been because relevant data had not been collected. In other words, the performance indicators did not match the stated objectives of the project and this reduced the impact and value of the evaluation.

Some evaluations did attempt to collect quantitative data directly relevant to widening participation. For example information on postcodes and fee waivers were recorded as indicators of socio-economic status for some 'taster' courses at Sheffield HallamUniversity, and year 9 students on an outreach programme run by the University of Sheffield were tracked through to entry to higher education institutions in Sheffield and elsewhere.

Many of the evaluations used participant response, usually collected through questionnaires. Falling somewhere between Morrison's (1993) 'illuminative' and 'survey' models of evaluation, this approach attempted to capture both the individual and unexpected responses of participants, and to gather some quantifiable data to match to targets. It was used for example to gather the views of young people from inner city schools visiting the university for the first time, and to evaluate the impact on older learners of 'taster' courses.

There were some practical problems in gathering the data. Post code residence of schoolchildren cannot be collected by the HE institution, for reasons of confidentiality, and so a less reliable proxy for social class, the location of the school, had to be used. While adults on taster courses were happy to reveal their post codes on a questionnaire, they were less willing to reveal other information. For example, only 30% of respondents answered a question on educational background. Questionnaires are relatively cheap and easy to administer, but do have serious limitations when personal information is sought from people who may be very reluctant to reveal what they perceive as their shortcomings.

While some of these evaluations offered valuable qualitative insights, they tended to be small-scale and diffuse in their design and choice of indicators, and so offered little opportunity to draw out general principles for successful practice. In some reports, specific and valuable recommendations for improvement were made but these had not been followed through to action. This argues for projects and activities to be more firmly located within institutional or departmental plans and targets, and for evaluations to be firmly linked at the design stage to these plans.

Key dimensions in planning evaluation

Choosing what to evaluate, whether to adopt a 'macro' or 'micro' approach, which methods to use and which indicators to select is a complex task, particularly if resources are limited. While acknowledging that no single approach will suit all circumstances, this section attempts to identify some critical factors to consider at the design stage, discusses these in relation to some of the relevant literature, and proposes a practical framework for planning.

First, it is proposed that the planning process for evaluating widening participation initiatives should consider how to build in these six dimensions:

* the capacity to **improve practice** as well as **proving** success
* **explicit values** relevant to widening participation
* **multi-purpose**
* **link to long-term and strategic planning** needs
* relevance to **stakeholder interests** beyond the institution
* the **value added** by collaborative processes.

Effecting change

Widening participation initiatives have a significant role to play in bringing about and embedding change. Evaluation has a role to play in this, through highlighting issues and acting as a catalyst for debate. To move beyond accountability and to act as a lever for change, the design will need to take account of multiple purposes and interests, a factor rarely acknowledged in the literature on evaluation. This may mean, for example, ensuring that the evaluation has relevance for different levels in the organisation and outside - senior management, faculty, the local community and local employers. While small scale evaluations cannot hope to address all interests, they can, as a minimum, relate to institutional objectives. Avoiding the parochialism that can attach to small-scale studies is critical if they are to have any influence.

Values

There is strong set of values underpinning widening participation strategies. At national policy level these are reflected in the importance attached to social inclusion, to change in institutional practice and to attitudinal change in communities and universities. The design of the evaluation should reflect these values, but in practice this can be difficult to achieve unless they are clearly identified at the outset. It is easy, for example, to identify participation in HE as desirable. It is not so easy to identify step changes in curriculum design, guidance or institutional culture which might also demonstrate a successful outcome. Two attempts to convert values into measurable outcomes illustrate the point. Writing about the evaluation of lifelong learning, Gelpi (1980) reflects values orientated towards democracy, equity and fairness. Although he was concerned with education in general and not higher education specifically, some of the criteria he proposes have particular relevance to social inclusion. Some examples he suggests are:

- participation of workers
- active participation of workers as teachers or facilitators
- introduction of folk culture as an integral part of formal curriculum
- participation of students in management.

Knapper and Cropley (2000), identify other criteria for evaluating lifelong learning that could be incorporated in institutional, departmental or faculty targets. These include:

- ease of student transfer between educational departments or 'streams'
- broad participation (by students, alumni etc) in decisions affecting education and management
- encouragement of research on lifelong learning.

These criteria address the need for flexibility, for democracy, and for using research as a means of knowledge creation, awareness-raising and learning through practice, all of which have relevance to widening participation. The problem with both, however, is locating them within the overall management and quality assurance processes in a university, and tying them to specific indicators and targets.

Monitoring and evaluation procedures

Practical guidelines on evaluation of widening participation initiatives offered by Woodrow *et al* (1998, 109) propose specific procedures to address a range of stakeholder interests:

- Setting targets and performance indicators for access as an integral part of institutions' overall monitoring processes.
- Profiling participants, including their socio-economic status, to insure that targeting policies are being implemented.
- Tracking participants through from their first involvement in the scheme to check their process in accessing HE.
- Tracking the post-HE entry progress of participants, including retention rates and reasons for any withdrawals, to check the long-term effectiveness of the scheme in preparing participants for HE.
- Monitoring reactions to the activities/programmes among participants, parents and partner institutions as a means of evaluating and improving the scheme.
- Evaluating the impact of the scheme on participating institutions, including the HEIs [Higher Education Institutions] as a means of assessing its wider influence.

In contrast to Gelpi's ideas, these guidelines explicitly link programmes to institutional commitment and values, and identify a number of easily measurable factors. There are some omissions which are relatively easy to measure, such as employability, and others, such as the evaluation of cultural change, or the place of academic research, which are important but harder to link to institutional targets.

A planning template

Work on the role of youth work in promoting social inclusion offers an approach to planning evaluation which has been adapted in this paper for widening participation initiatives (DfEE; 1999; 36). It groups performance indicators into three categories:

1. **process and outputs** (e.g. percentage of target population reached, number of initial contacts converted into project participants and number regularly using project);

2. **outcomes and effectiveness** (e.g. numbers gaining employment or training, participating in FE or achieving qualifications or awards)

3. **Inputs and efficiency** (e.g. cost per positive outcome, income from external sources).

Linking indicators to the three stages of a programme's life - input, process and output - offers a practical template for planning the evaluation of both large and small-scale initiatives. It encourages a focus on measurable indicators, incorporates process, and allows for the development of a 'value added' approach.

Value added and the 'value chain'

The success of widening participation initiatives often depends on the contribution of partners outside the university, and this may bring unexpected benefits. For example, a higher education 'taster' day planned in conjunction with a group of schools may bring benefits beyond the immediate event, such as ideas for future collaboration, or links with the wider local community. While the value added through the process of collaboration is often acknowledged, it is rarely included in evaluations. An approach using the concept of the 'value chain', developed for evaluating services to communities (Sanderson, 1998) and used in a proposed framework for evaluating 'learning cities' in the UK (DfEE, 1999), attempts to address this deficit. This analyses the key stages at which value may be added in the planning, management and delivery of a community-based service and can be used as the basis of a staged evaluation.

A proposed framework

Drawing on all of the above sources, this chapter proposes a framework for planning the evaluation of widening participation projects and initiatives. It gives examples of a range of indicators to support monitoring, tracking and evaluation and links them to three stages in the life cycle of an initiative. Evaluation at the 'input' stage is mainly concerned with successful targetting, at the 'process' or implementation stage the focus is on improving quality, and at the 'outcomes' stage, it is about assessing efficiency and effectiveness. The indicators are examples only and would need to be adapted for individual initiatives or projects.

Methods are not detailed in the framework, but clearly, this approach does lend itself to a closed and structured methodology, rather than to, say, an action research model. It does not exclude the use of qualitative data, however. While the 'input' stage would require mainly quantitative data, qualitative approaches could be incorporated in the process evaluation and outcomes stages. It is also possible to convert some qualitative data to measurable outcomes even where elusive concepts such as attitudes are the focus: opinion polls routinely do exactly this. If the purpose of the evaluation is to effect change, choice between methods is a matter of balance: what an evaluation loses in richness and authenticity, it may gain in its capacity to influence. The value of combining quantitative and qualitative methods, what Richardson (1996) calls 'methodological eclecticism' is well established in the research literature (see, for example, Bryman, 1998, 1992; Morrison, ibid; Wilcox, 1992; Bell, 1993; Cohen and Manion, 1994). Two very useful techniques for evaluation, triangulation and progressive focusing, depend on such an approach, and can easily be defended in terms of their validity.

In addition, the scope, indicators and methods used will be guided by other practical considerations. For example:

- What *resources* are available (collecting and using qualitative data is more time-consuming, for example)?
- Which indicators and methods are easiest to apply?
- Are there any *'core'* widening participation indicators which should be universally applied across the project or institution? (e.g. social class indicators?)
- Which indicators are more suitable for small scale *qualitative* evaluations or research projects?
- How do they align with *institutional or national indicators* already used in use (e.g. data collected on enrolment forms)?
- How do they support the evaluation of institutional policy?

The contribution of research

This chapter has addressed the issue of evaluation, but would be incomplete without some reference to research. Research has an important role to play in creating knowledge and informing debate in this area of policy and practice. In fact, performance indicators based on the amount of research money spent or papers published could be included in an evaluation strategy. Regrettably, although there have been many research projects and surveys in areas linked to widening participation (notably adult learning and continuing education) there is far less which is linked to government policy or institutional change. While it is easy to guess at some reasons for this - lack of funding and its relatively recent rise on institutional and national agendas for example - this is not the whole story. Much research in related areas focuses on the individual in the education system. There is relatively little on the social context of class or educational purpose and little on the experience of young adults.

John Field (1999) highlights this deficit in looking at research into adult participation.
While acknowledging the wealth of material in this area, he laments the lack of support from
policy-makers in extending the scale of such research, pointing to several gaps. In particular,
he identifies the individualistic focus of much research, which leads to a 'life history' approach,
and which fails to take account of social capital models of lifelong learning and participation.
A human capital model lends itself more easily to some kinds of research, and, Field suggests,
may also be more attractive to those who fund or commission it:

> 'Human capital theory finds favour with policy-makers because it is easily measured;
> investments in individual skills and qualifications lead on to identifiable returns to
> the individual; the assumption is that these investments and returns are not only
> good for the individual, but for the whole community. Yet much learning is social in
> nature, and many of the returns are only realised when new capacities are applied
> collectively' (Field, ibid:12).

For many engaged in developing widening participation policy and practice, these social
values are critical and need to inform research topics and perspectives. Practice has moved
beyond the adult returner and access courses as a response to equity issues, and research needs
to reflect these changes and offer new insights.

Conclusion

This chapter has been about making effective use of the evaluation of widening participation
strategies. It argues for a more consistent focus on measurable targets related to social inclusion,
for evaluation to be taken as seriously at the planning stage as the activities and projects
themselves, and for a coherent approach which makes connections with the national, local
and institutional agendas. The rationale for this approach is its capacity to influence the
uncommitted and bring about change.

If evaluation is to improve practice, then more of the processes and outcomes need to be
shared. This does not have to be confined to conferences and paper publications, which tend
to focus on research, but could be web-based, and support dialogue and debate on approaches
and findings as they develop. The University of North London's website on social inclusion
cited earlier is a good start on this.

Finally, while the focus of this chapter has been on evaluation, some gaps in research into widening participation have been noted. To help 'join up' the thinking in a field of practice which is often marginalised, there is a need for more policy driven research, especially to look at issues relating to cultural change and the extent to which the government's social inclusion agenda is being met.

References

Bell, J, (1993) *Doing Your Research Project: A Guide for First-Time Researchers in Education and Social Science* 2nd ed., Buckingham, Open University Press.

Bryman, A. (1988) *Quantity and Quality in Social Research* London, Unwin Hyman.

Bryman, A. (1992) Quantitative and qualitative research: Further reflections on their integration. In J. Brannen (Ed) *Mixing Methods: Quantitative and qualitative research, Aldershot, Avebury Press.*

Cohen, L. and Mannion, L. (1994) *Research Methods in Education* 4th ed., London, Routledge.

Dearing, R. (1997) *Higher Education and the Learning Society,* National Committee of Enquiry into Higher Education, London, HMSO.

DfEE (1999) *Moving on Up: how youth work raises achievement and promotes social inclusion,* Nottingham, Department for Education and Employment.

DfEE (1999) *Practice, Progress and Value. Learning communities: assessing what value they add,* London, Department for Education and Employment.

Gelpi, E. (1980) Politics and lifelong education policies and practice in Cropley, A.J. (ed.) *Towards a system of lifelong education,* Oxford, Pergamon.

Field, J.(1999) 'Participation under the magnifying glass' in *Adults Learning,* Leicester, National Institute for Adult and Continuing Education, Vol. 11, No.3, 12-13.

Higher Education Funding Council for England (1999) *Performance indicators in higher education.* Circular 99/66 Bristol, HEFCE.

Knapper, K. and Cropley, A.J. (2000) *Lifelong learning in higher education* 3rd edition, London, Kogan Page

Morrison, K. (1993) *Planning and accomplishing school-centred evaluation* Dereham, Norfolk, Peter Francis.

Richardson, J. T. E. (1996) *Handbook of Qualitative Research Methods for Psychology and the Social Sciences* Leicester, The British Psychological Society, 167.

Roper, B., Ross,A. and Thomson, D. (2000) *'Let's really measure the value of higher education'*
Guardian Education, 2 May.

Sanderson, I.(1998) *Made to measure - evaluation in practice in local government,* London,
Local Government Training Board.

Wilcox, B. (1992) *Time constrained evaluation: a practical approach for LEAs and schools*
London, Routledge

Woodrow, M. (1998) From Elitism to Inclusion, London, CVCP

Notes

[1] By the Higher Education Statistics Agency (HESA). See www.hes.ac.uk for details

[2] For further details of the methodology and an on-line discussion, see www.unl.ac.uk/mco/
social inclusion

[3] HEFCE Regional Widening Participation Project, Yorkshire and Humberside, 1999/00.

Chapter Five

Finnish summer universities: educational equality and lifelong learning

Ellen Piesanen

Finnish summer universities as a part of the Finnish educational system

Finnish summer universities have a long tradition, with roots going back to the 19th century, when the University of Helsinki offered various summer courses also open to other than its regular students. In the beginning of the last century the instruction offered by the summer universities involved mainly the updating and further education of teachers, thus giving teachers a chance, outside term time in summer, to improve their professional competencies. A summer university delivered its instruction locally, usually in accordance with the syllabuses of the University of Helsinki. Currently there are 21 summer universities in Finland and they function on the educational market as an important educational forum of lifelong learning.

The 1960s, 1970s and 1980s in particular saw a rapid expansion of the Finnish university system. Many of the universities founded at the time were established in localities that had a summer university. In this way the summer university system was fostering educational equality, its very existence serving to promote educational, regional and social equality. When the regular university system was extended to various parts of the country, the role of the summer universities changed.

The summer universities operate in the field of adult education. They deliver, on the one hand, *open university instruction*[1] that accords with the degree requirements of the regular universities and, on the other hand, *vocational courses and seminars*. In addition to instruction proper, there are various language studies, and courses on Finnish and Finnish culture aimed at immigrants. Gradually the range of instruction has come to include courses preparing general upper secondary school leavers for the entrance examinations of universities or other higher education establishments, as well as university studies for the third age and Studia Generalia lectures open to the general public. In addition summer universities organise local and national cultural events in collaboration with other European organisations, more broad-based events. Because of the nature of their instructional provision, they function, in an area somewhere between the regular university system (eg open university instruction and the provision of further education) and liberal adult education (interest-based and language studies and lectures).

The foci of their teaching provision vary between different summer universities, largely depending on local conditions such as the nearness or remoteness of a regular university, the conditions on the local labour market and so on. However, in most cases the emphasis lies on open university instruction, with vocational and professional further education courses and the like representing a smaller in some cases a minimal proportion of the given institution's total educational provision. However, there are summer universities whose existence is made possible solely by such courses, as these are often financially more profitable. This is because they are often paid for by employers, such as local authorities or enterprises, which makes it more likely that there will be enough students for the course to be delivered.

The current situation of the educational market ensures that the quality of the education or training provided - including open university instruction and vocational and professional further education - must be high. The clients - the parties ordering a course or the students themselves - demand value for their money. Because of this, the summer universities' annual educational provision must be up to date and, where there is competition, actually more current than that offered in other institutions. Because of their flexibility and the broad range of operational modes available to them, the summer universities have a good chance of achieving this aim.

The administration and operational model of Finnish summer universities

The summer universities are maintained by local associations and certain regional councils. Today they operate all the year round even if the emphasis is still on the provision and delivery of the summer courses. Their operations are financed with fees payable by the students, in addition to grants from the state and the local authorities. The summer universities function in close collaboration with the regular Finnish universities and many other partners (local authorities, enterprises, associations) also cooperate with them.

The summer universities' operational model is flexible and involves a minimum of organisational structures, which allows them to offer an extensive and varied range of teaching.

59

An important aspect of their operations is a conscious endeavour to serve the needs of their own region. Thus the summer universities operate on the local level, being based all around Finland. This operational model enables them to cater for a very diverse range of clients. Anyone can follow the instruction offered because applicants are not subject to any requirements regarding age or previous education. As a result, the range of educational provision is similarly very varied and covers a very broad range of fields of study, representing very diverse levels of the educational system. Because of this wide-ranging educational provision, the summer universities can also target groups with no other access to education.

Finnish summer universities within markets of lifelong learning

Lifelong learning is a learning strategy where studying - either within the formal education system or elsewhere - at different stages of their life is, in one way or another, a part of an individual's whole life course (OECD 1996, 1998). Accordingly, implementing the principle of lifelong learning poses the educational system as a whole and adult education in particular with serious challenges. On the one hand there is a quantitative rise in educational demand, on the other hand the educational system is expected to offer more individualised educational alternatives. This presupposes a broader range of educational options and, above all, more flexible educational arrangements. The Finnish model of summer universities is one example of such organisation of educational provision.

Particularly in industrialised countries, the educational level of the population continues to rise, which means that in the society of the future the aging will include a greater proportion of more highly educated people than before. Demand for education for the third age increases with a corresponding expectation of higher quality. While today's university-level instruction for the aging comprises largely general lectures, in the future there may be increasing demands for a more versatile approach, including a scientific or scholarly perspective. Third-age studies may also become more degree-oriented, with the result that more people may be taking parts of university degree programmes and even completing degrees after they have left working life proper. This may be assumed to increasingly affect, in the future, the operations of the Open University and, through it, those of summer universities.

The university-level instruction delivered by the summer universities will become an even more important factor than before because many of the barriers described above can be lowered by channelling some of lifelong learning into the activities of the Open University.

The Open University can offer study opportunities to people of various ages and with various levels of education. In addition, using the methods of multiform teaching and distance education the Open University operates over a broad-based network and even virtually, all factors that make studies possible in the most varied life situations. This fact has been recognised in, among other things, a report by a Finnish committee on lifelong learning, where the Open University is mentioned as an aspect of a national strategy of lifelong learning (Committee Report 1997).

Finnish summer universities as promoters of social equality

The structures of contemporary society, the emphasis on individualisation and the goal of lifelong learning, set those planning and delivering education new kinds of challenge. The feasibility of either full-time or part-time studying varies from one life situation to another, and in many cases it is open studying, both studies at the Open University and open instruction on other levels of the educational system, that can open a individual to completely novel ways of achieving their educational goals.

At its best, the educational provision of the summer universities represents the criteria associated with open educational systems. The advantage of open educational systems lies in the equal opportunities that they, in principle, offer to all people entering education, thus creating social equality. For example, in various parts of the world open learning options have improved the educational opportunities available to homekeeping women (Evans 1994).

What is the potential of the Finnish summer university system to promote social equality and lessen inequality, particularly as regards access to higher education? In terms of higher education policy, the summer university can be seen as an important forum for implementing individual-centred operational principles. The subject may be considered from the perspective not only of regional equality but also that of promotion of educational and, indirectly, social equality.

Regional equality

The fact that the summer universities operate locally and are consequently able to promote lifelong learning on the regional level may be considered a special feature of the summer universities. In a sparsely populated country this is an important factor promoting regional equality. In some cases, mainly when they have a broad catchment area, summer universities function much more widely than inside the municipality where they are primarily based.

The importance of the summer university network is particularly marked in the north of Finland, Lapland, where distances are long and journeys laborious. The network makes it possible to provide instruction in the smaller towns and municipalities. In some regions the nearest regular university is also channelling some of its teaching provision through the summer university network, an arrangement known as the Provincial University System. This ensures adequate enrolment, difficult to achieve, particularly in the less common subjects, through the instructional provision of a summer university alone.

The activities of the Open Universities derive largely from a conception of learning based on self-directedness (eg Rowntree 1992; Bell & Tight 1993; Koro 1993). Self-directedness has been the starting point for, among other things, many teaching models and methods that have come to serve needs linked with individualisation: part-time teaching, distance education, flexibility, accessibility. Thus, apart from traditional contact teaching (such as lectures and seminars), open university instruction is delivered also as distance learning. Distance learning methods in particular make it possible also to reach those students who have limited opportunities to visit the municipalities where the summer universities are based. The utilisation potential of the virtual university is also improving rapidly, another factor increasing people's access to tertiary-level instruction in their home area or nearby. Because of new information technologies are being increasingly used in the delivery of Open University instruction, a nationwide tutor network is being constructed to support this system (Ministry of Education 2000).

Educational equality

The Open University courses offered by the summer universities are taught mainly at evenings and weekends, enabling working people to take up such studies. Given that, in addition, access to Open University studies is free, irrespective of educational background, the summer universities are able to contribute to educational equality. Accordingly, research on the Open University (Piesanen 1996, 1988, 1999a, 1999b) has revealed that students can use it as a testing arena where they may try out, not only their own abilities but also their chosen subject and the nature of university studies in general. These are important factors; in positive cases they have helped students to eventually enter university as regular students.

The most important aspect of this particular function of Open University studies is that in the Open University students gain a good picture of the academic disciplines they study there. Making up one's mind about whether one wishes to enter regular university is a long-term decision. If the chosen subject proves to be a wrong choice, one's studies may be prolonged or one may drop out of university altogether. This may in turn have consequences both on the individual level and on the level of higher education policy-making.

In the testing arena thus provided by the Open University, young people can also prove their abilities as university students. Feeling successful in one's Open University studies may be due to three factors: one's personal abilities on the one hand and finding the style of university studies and the nature of university education congenial on the other. Students are able to find out whether they really like university education. They can also ascertain whether such studies would be too theoretical and demanding for them.

Another factor promoting educational equality is what is termed the Open University Route: after completing approximately a third of a degree programme at the Open University a student can be admitted as a regular university student. This applies also to the older mature students, similarly able to use their open university studies as a means of testing their abilities and the nature of university education.

Summer universities also create educational equality also by opening access to higher education to people who may not have been able to enter it through the usual channels. According to research findings (Piesanen 1999a), open university instruction also improves the chances of entering higher education among those who were less successful at school.

Social equality

The function of the summer universities as potential promoters of both regional and educational equality is reflected in their potential to improve social equality among the adult population. Research has revealed that in many cases, studies at the Open University have been felt to affect perceptions of social equality. Some of the students believe that Open University studies will help them find a better job and thus achieve higher status.

Open University studies also have a social function among unemployed students. The opportunity to take up studies when one has neither a job nor a student place is important in itself. In such a situation, studying at the Open University may help the unemployed person to structure their life and give it meaning, thus reducing the risk of marginalisation and relieving feelings of inequality. All these are factors in the improvement of social status and the reduction of inequality, which may check the emergence of disparities between social groups or their deepening.

From the student's point of view, the greatest obstacles are linked with student fees: the vocational and professional further education is often paid for by employers, while on the other hand the individual student must pay fees for academic open university courses. These fees are often relatively high, especially from the viewpoint of unemployed students. Thus, in some cases the cost of summer university education can become a factor limiting educational equality.

Further, completing extensive modules of degree-oriented studies in addition to working is a long-term project that may take several years, with some degree of drop-out unavoidable. This often impairs the student's motivation. Moreover, to the student, prolonged studies and dropping out are also financial disappointments.

The various forms of financial aid for students and the ways in which the relevant regulations are applied are one factor influencing how far the less well off are actually able to make use of the education offered by the summer universities. Removing economic obstacles is highly desirable because in most cases education has purely positive effects from the perspective both of an individual's mastery of their life and of their future educational and employment status. (Piesanen 1996.)

However, the provision of academic open university studies is not the only means of promoting lifelong learning, preventing social exclusion and fostering regional, educational and social equality. The further vocational and professional training and upgrading courses (some of them academic) and course-form training for the unemployed delivered by the summer universities can also contribute.

Evaluating the operation of the summer universities

In recent years, evaluation of education has become an important tool for developing the educational system. Evaluation is intended to produce data that the various parties - political decision-makers, education providers, teaching staff etc - can draw on as they seek to develop their own activities so that these will optimally serve the goals set for education. Accordingly, in evaluating the operation of educational institutions effectiveness is seen as a central consideration, the starting point being to assess how far the goals set for the given activity have been achieved.

Like other education providers, Finnish summer universities have been obliged to conduct quantitative evaluation in order to maintain their activities: annual statistics have been compiled both on the financial aspects of their operations and on the provision and delivery of instruction. This year has been the start of the qualitative evaluation of the summer universities using a method termed External Self-Evaluation (Välimaa 2000).

The groundwork for the self-evaluation project was done in the University of Jyväskylä, at the Institute for Educational Research, and all Finnish summer universities will assess their own activities in the course of this autumn (2000). Each summer university will consider the various thematic areas important for and central to its activities and then present a report as its self-assessment. A number of areas have emerged as central, from the perspective of developing the operations of the summer universities; they include many administrative questions linked with making and implementing decisions, questions linked with the planning, marketing and delivery of instruction, and questions linked with the organisation of financial management as well as staff development, flexibility and their 'social space'.

It will be interesting to see how the various summer universities - different in terms both of their regional characteristics and of their teaching provision - will assess the quality of their operations and what kind of opportunities they will perceive for developing them. This will also generate information on how the summer universities themselves see their contribution in the arena of lifelong learning and how they, in their individual areas of activity, seek to achieve the goals originally set for their operation, for example as regards the promotion of social equality and the reduction of inequality.

Conclusion

Finnish society is marked by strong optimism about education, and in the last few years education has become more important than ever. It is considered an important resource not only from the perspective of intellectual growth among the population but also from that of the economic growth of the nation. The function of the educational market is to satisfy the educational needs of various parties. Another characteristic feature of today's society is its strong privatisation, an emphasis on individuality. Accordingly, individualistic perspectives have become more prominent in various sectors of society, not least in educational demand. Like that of other types of educational establishment, the position of summer universities as a part of the Finnish educational system can be examined from the perspective of *individualism* and *market forces*, two aspects of *modern society* (Clark 1983; Giddens 1987, 1991, 1996; Beck 1992; Beck, Giddens & Lash 1994; Marginson 1997.) The strong influence exerted by market forces both on political decision-making, operations and their implementation and on the individual's choices and decisions is linked with *individualisation*. According to Beck (1992), individualisation refers to a situation where individuals operating in the various fields of life are dependent on the existing markets. This applies, apart from various choices involved in daily consumption, also to choices concerning working life and education.

As regards the summer universities, they are a students' market where students operate as a real market force, making their choices from a range of educational provision freely available to them and paying for it. In this way demand influences, the nature of educational provision. However, the greatest threat facing the activities of the summer universities is the fierce competition on the educational marketplace, which has already forced some summer universities to target their educational provision at a broader range of potential students and at the same time to design it to more precise specifications. Competition is intense: open university instruction is offered not only by the Open Universities but also by many adult education centres and folk high schools, often based in the same locality as a summer university. Also the number of establishments providing vocational adult education has similarly increased very considerably in the last few years.

Universities have traditionally been elitist institutions serving the needs of the upper classes. In Finland, as elsewhere, the situation has changed noticeably in the last few decades. In Finland the contributing factors have been particularly the expansion of the university network, the introduction of the Open University and the setting up of the AMK (vocational higher education) institutions. At present, some 67 per cent of the age cohort in Finland enters tertiary-level education at the same time as Open University has a yearly enrolment of some 80,000 students, some of which study at summer universities.

Similarly, a consideration of the educational system from the perspective of lifelong education, including the older or even the aged citizen, shows that access to tertiary-level instruction is easier than ever and that the volume of educational provision is broadening all the time. This increasing provision also makes it possible to target, better than before, groups that still find it difficult to gain entry to education of this kind. Such groups include the unemployed, people living beyond easy communications, immigrants, and so on. Accordingly, there are many potential students in the adult population able and willing to participate in higher education if only they are given an opportunity to do so.

The Finnish summer university network, originally a system for the further education of teachers in summer, has since developed into a broad-based round-the-year activity. Despite Finland having both a comprehensive system of universities and AMK institutions and a wide-ranging network of vocational education institutions and liberal adult education organisations, the summer universities have carved themselves a niche and developed further there.

At the moment their most central role in achieving equality is an educational one. Educational provision - including the teaching provision of the summer universities - is nearer at hand than it used to be. Open University instruction makes it possible to conduct university-level studies 'anywhere': in almost all municipalities, almost anyone can engage in studies at almost any time. It depends on the individual student how they will make use of their studies. They can use them as vocational or professional further education but also as a means of gaining access to a regular university, either by taking part in the regular student selection process or by taking the Open University Route described above. The summer universities can cater for very diverse clients, including groups with access to little or no other educational provision, and also those at risk of marginalisation, such as the unemployed, people with inadequate basic education and immigrants. Unemployed students can enroll both for academic/general studies and on vocational courses. Immigrants are offered language instruction for example. In all, the Finnish summer university system, which provides not only academic open university instruction and vocational and professional training but also interest-related and cultural activities representing liberal adult education, is a welfare-state service intended to improve equality among citizens, whether in regional, educational or social terms. Moreover, the system has shown that it has every prospect of also meeting these goals.

References

Beck, U. (1992) *Risk Society: Towards a New Modernity*. London, SAGE Publications.

Beck, U., Giddens, A. & Lash, S. (1994). *Reflexive Modernization. Politics, Tradition and Aesthetics in the Modern Social Order*. Cambridge, Polity Press.

Bell, R. & Tight, M. (1993) *Open Universities: A British Tradition?* Buckingham: The Society for Research into Higher Education & Open University Press.

Clark, B. R. (1983) *The Higher Education System. Academic Organization in Cross-national Perspective*. Berkely, Los Angeles, London, University of California Press.

Committee Report (1997) *The Joy of Learning : A National Strategy for Lifelong Learning*. Helsinki, Ministry of Education, 14.

Evans, T. (1994) *Understanding Learners in Open and Distance Education*. Open and distance learning series. London, Kogan Page.

Giddens, A. (1987) *Social Theory and Modern Sociology*. Cambridge, Polity Press.

Giddens, A. (1991) *Modernity and Self identity. Self and Society in the Late Modern Age*. Cambridge, Polity Press.

Giddens, A. (1996) *Modernitetens Följder*. Lund, Studentlitteratur.

Koro, J. (1993) *Aikuinen oman oppimisensa ohjaajana*. Jyväskylän yliopisto, Jyväskylä studies in education, psychology and social research 98.

Marginson, S. (1997) *Markets in Eduction*. St. Leonards, Allen & Unwin.

Ministry of Education 2000, *Higher Education Policy in Finland*, Ministry of Education, Helsinki.

OECD (1996) *Lifelong Learning for All: Meeting of the Education Committee at Ministerial Level, 16-17 January 1996*, OECD, Paris.

OECD, Centre for Educational Research and Innovation (1998) *Education Policy Analysis 1998*, OECD, Paris.

Piesanen, E. (1996) *The Role of Open University in the Development of Young Adults' Career Perspectives* (in Finnish with English summary), Institute for Educational Research Publication Series A, Research Reports 67, University of Jyväskylä, Institute for Educational Research, Jyväskylä.

Piesanen, E. (1998) 'A Finnish Open University as Young Adults' Testing Arena', *Higher Education Management* 10 (3), 137-151.

Piesanen, E. (1999a) *Open University in Finland and the Development of Under-25 Students' Educational and Working Career* (in Finnish with English summary), Institute for Educational Research Occasional Papers 7, University of Jyväskylä, Institute for Educational Research, Jyväskylä.

Piesanen, E. (1999b). *The Open University on the Markets of an Increasingly Individualised Society: A Bargaining Chip in Educational and Labour Market Polices or an Opportunity for the Young Adult?* (in Finnish with English summary), Institute for Educational Research, Research Reports 8, University of Jyväskylä, Institute for Educational Research, Jyväskylä.

Rowntree, D. (1992) *Exploring Open and Distance Learning.* Open and distance learning series. London: Kogan Page.

Välimaa, J. (2000) Ulkoinen itsearviointi ja käyttötypologiat. (External self-evaluation and practical typologies.) In Honkimäki, S. and Jalkanen, H. (ed.) *Innovatiivinen yliopisto?* (Innovative University?) University of Jyväskylä. Institute for Educational Research, Jyväskylä.

Note

[1] In Finland the Open University is a decentralised system within which regular universities and other educational institutions, such as adult education establishments and *summer universities*, give students, irrespective of their educational background or where they live, an opportunity to study parts of the regular university degree programmes. The Open University offers an extensive range of courses and examinations but confers no degrees. After having completed approximately a third of a degree programme students have the option of entering university as regular students.

Chapter Six

Ethnicity and higher education in South Africa: evaluating the process of change

Devi Jajab

Introduction

South African constitutions, prior to the new democratic dispensation, were premised on inequality and steadfast commitment to white supremacy. The apartheid policy in law and application systematically discriminated against black people in all aspects of social and educational life. The deep scars of this appalling programme are still visible in our society today.

The end result is a society where inequality is one of the defining characteristics. This is reflected in all the key elements which impact on the quality of life such as nutrition and health; illiteracy and education; infant mortality and life expectancy, wealth and poverty and others. In terms of the Gini coefficient, South Africa is one of the countries having the highest measure of inequality amongst its citizens.

In the light of this, South Africa's smooth transition into a non-racist democracy has been hailed widely as nothing short of a miracle. The world remains captivated by the dramatic collapse of the apartheid regime and the emergence of a democracy after 48 years of Nationalist rule.

The South African higher education context

The Nationalist government through its policy of apartheid in education restricted access to schooling and post-secondary education according to race and ethnic origin and in so doing, imposed a system of separate education characterised by extreme inequalities. It also effectively built barriers around racial groups creating strangers among learners.

According to Griesel in her report *Access and the Tertiary Education Sector* (2000), two sets of legislation shaped the provision of education, namely:

1. The Bantu Education Act of 1953 that restructured formal schooling along racial and ethnic lines and the Extension of University Education Act of 1957 that applied the same ideology to higher education.

2. The Separate Universities Act of 1980 gave rise to the establishment of ethnic universities in the homelands for specific racial and ethnic groups. In the late 1970s and early 1980s, the establishment of technikons alongside training colleges and universities followed.

The challenge faced by the new government was to build a coherent system out of a deeply fragmented higher education sector made up of 21 universities, 15 technikons and a vast number of colleges previously controlled by three ministries and a range of departments.

In summary, the contextual challenges of the early 1990s required a framework and sets of legislation that would among other things:

*   bring into a single coherent national framework all institutions (technikons, universities and colleges) operating in the higher education sector;
*   broaden access to meet the society's development needs and to ensure access of those previously excluded[1]
*   regulate quality and efficiency
*   increase institutional capacity towards massification and diversity
*   create a globally competitive skilled population as rapidly as possible.

Central to the transformation process were the issues of equity and redress in access particularly of African students. A decade later some have claimed that the access debate has deepened and shifted.[2]

Transformation of higher education in South Africa

South Africa's ANC-led Government is presently grappling with the transformation of higher education. At the first cabinet meeting of the new government, President Thabo Mbeki posed the question: Is our education system on the road to the 21st century? Given the investment of public funds in higher education, the South African public must have a vital interest in the answer. The White Paper of 1997 established a comprehensive and ambitious transformation agenda to harness higher education to overcome social inequities, contribute to reconstruction and development and enable South Africa to engage effectively with globalization. But, transformation is being viewed from different perspectives by major players. On the one hand the government's understanding is premised on democratic justice and issues of redress and redistribution designed to address historical inequities of race, class and gender. This requires radical change in the make up of the student body, staff of universities and curriculum.[3] On the other hand the corporate world views transformation as aligned to market forces and the pursuit of profit. Here transformation becomes synonymous with restructuring, containing expenditure and increasing productivity. In order to satisfy the needs of an export driven economy, universities must be transformed into lean and mean producers of informational content and profitable skills. In addition the pressure to switch from traditional academic education to occupation oriented training systems is an attempt to address the skills shortage in the country. South African universities are currently reeling under these competing pressures.

Another set of tensions exist between the formerly 'ethnic institutions' (historically disadvantaged institutions) and the white institutions (historically advantaged institutions). Six years after the end of apartheid, black academics argue that the bulk of the billions in government subsidies have gone to former white institutions which were privileged in the past, while the former black institutions which supported the liberation movements and opened their doors to financially needy students received a pittance. Declining subsidies, dwindling enrolments and rising student debt, could with a variety of management problems plague many of the former 'bush universities'. The former black universities, some of which are almost bankrupt and kept afloat by massive overdrafts, expected the democratic government to treat them with sympathy. Many claim the opposite has happened[4].

For others who were able to cross the divide between the past and present, the issues have far wider implications[5]. According to Ramphele[6] first black vice-chancellor of the University of Cape Town, (a historically white institution), attempts by the government to transform the grossly inequitable and inadequate school system in South Africa are characterised by failure to translate good policies into sound practice. The tendency for policy makers, for political reasons, to disregard the extent of the devastation of 40 years of dysfunctional education will mean that they will simply ignore the deep scars and focus on equity in education. The importance of acknowledging the scars is, according to Ramphele, a necessary condition for developing appropriate strategies to manage the transition to a better education for all.

The Higher Education Act promulgated in December 1997, while affirming and entrenching the role of students in institutional governance, has been curtailed by economic realities and policies put in place to address broader transformation issues at a national level. Despite affirmative action policies and programmes, major subsidy cuts in education generally and tertiary education in particular have meant that previously disadvantaged students are effectively excluded from education on financial grounds. Many tertiary institutions are currently embroiled in conflict against management over admission of financially needy students. There is widespread disillusionment among student leaders who believe the management at universities are uncaring and inflexible and that the national government has reneged on promises made during the liberation struggle. However, progress since the adoption of the White Paper has been extremely mixed and uneven according to the Council of Higher Education Report (1998-1999). Very positive trends coexist with greatly worrying conditions and developments. Overall, a great deal more has to be accomplished if higher education is to be a system of and for the 21st century.

The status of higher education is inextricably bound to the feeder school system from whence its student cohorts emerge. From this point of view, higher education inherited many problems that have emanated from the school system. Briefly these translate as follows:

1. South African youth are early starters - they are generally active in politics from the age of 12. The high school leadership for example of predominantly black youth was instrumental in the mass uprisings against apartheid rule. Their famous slogan 'liberation before education' supported by the ANC in exile, impacted directly on school violence, burning of books and classrooms and produced a culture of learning that was demand based on a notion of entitlement. The 1976 Soweto riots where youth led the vanguard against apartheid education is commemorated in post apartheid South Africa as a national youth day on the 16th June. For black youth then the school system was to all intents and purposes a political playground in which they actively fought for their rights. In contrast Indian and Coloured youth did not use education as a weapon against apartheid. They accepted, albeit, under protest the separate education meted to them and progressed under the system. It is important to note that they did receive a hierachically better education than the black child as more money was spent on the coloured and Indian

child than the black child.

2. South African youth were segregated from pre-school to tertiary level along racial and ethnic lines. Separate ministries of education were established for each racial group with budgets determined on a racial sliding scale. It is not surprising therefore that at tertiary institutions although they share common physical spaces, they, according to Naidoo[7], do not share the same socio-psychological space. In the so-called liberal white institutions, white students do not relate comfortably with their black peers and vice versa. It is a common sight to see students of different racial groups playing cards or pool or having lunch with their own group members. Cross group relationships are rare on South African campuses.

3. Bantu education discouraged and in some cases, prevented the teaching of maths and science in most schools[8]. Accordingly, black students at tertiary institutions are ghettoised in the humanities. For those in the sciences the attrition rate is very high.

4. Most teachers who are products of Bantu education have huge skills gap not on account of their lack of intelligence but rather on account of a lack of opportunity. There is little support from tertiary institutions to upgrade their skills.

5. An added complication to the quality of teaching staff is the breakdown of discipline during the struggle. Poor morale, intimidation by comrades and "comtsotsis" in the early 70s to the late 90s wreaked havoc on the remaining dedicated teachers. Teachers are literally afraid of their students.

6. Area studies reveal that there is widespread abuse of alcohol by teachers during school hours, as well as absenteeism. Some are either holding other jobs outside the school system or studying full-time elsewhere.

Accordingly, the South African Students' Congress (SASCO) has challenged tertiary institutions on legal grounds, on two issues:

I   exclusion from admission on financial grounds
II exclusion (in some cases) on financial grounds with poor academic performance.

Although institutions have differed in their strategies to combat the crisis, they appear to stand firm on the issue of a culture of non-payment, which threatens their very survival. Their resoluteness has the strong backing of government.

Throughout the country, sporadic protests have been staged in the form of marches, violence and damage to property. In some instances, institutions have had to cease lectures and close their doors as temporary measures in attempting to seek resolutions. But, despite the disruptions to classes, more insidious changes are taking place, which will have longer-term impact on institutional dynamics. They are as follows:

- Polarisation of students along racial, ethnic, socio-economic and political lines.
- According to Bhengu of the National Youth Commission[9], the majority of disadvantaged students happen to be Black Africans as opposed to so called Coloured and Indians. For example at least 20% of African youth live in shacks and another 9% in huts. In contrast nearly all white, coloured and Asian youth live in houses or apartments. Only 47% of young Africans live in homes with electricity and only 36% in homes with running water. The products of separate institutions in the immediate past, currently, each group does not fully understand the other's reality. This is already translating into problems at student governance levels where suspicion, mistrust and conflict are rife. Black African students have been viewed as being more problematic by administration than their more privileged fellow students.
- The issue of class and privilege has become a divisive factor at tertiary institutions today as the concerns of financial aid students differ radically from self- funding students.
- The monopolisation of black students in the residences poses special problems for diversity initiatives.

The current realities of the South African institutions of higher learning today test the limits of all involved in education, academic support and administration. As post-apartheid tertiary institutions make their transition from racially separate to open centres of learning, they bring within their fold a culturally diverse population of students and staff hitherto unknown to each other. Differing in socio-political realities, environmental experiences, educational needs and expectations, their impact on the nature and quality of student services is significant. Under-prepared, emotionally traumatised students need specialised educational and counselling support. In addition, the ethnic and racial diversity of the student population raises issues of cultural sensitivity and relevance. The diversity in the student population calls for a radical restructuring of conventional student support systems in financial aid, residences, health, career and curriculum advising and student counselling. In addition, the need for specialists trained to work sensitively with diversity along gender, disability, sexual orientation and other aspects, is essential. The challenge to the historically white institutions, in the educational process is to address both equity and excellence.

The educational process as a matter of necessity has to address the learning histories of students and the consequent nature of under preparedness and preparedness in the classroom context. In addressing the learning needs of under prepared students two central foci have been identified:

A language focus

The development of competence in the medium of instruction of an educational institution is clearly important in enabling students to engage effectively in the learning - teaching process. The medium of instruction at all South African tertiary institutions is English or Afrikaans. The recommendation to introduce African languages has been mooted but not implemented.

A cognitive focus

The nature of discourse of formal scientific knowledge is deeply embedded in the tradition of western scientific thought. According to Leatt (1992), the epistemic assumptions which underpin this historic trajectory are very different from those which have developed within an indigenous (to Africa) trajectory. An educational system that accommodates and acknowledges the cultural realities of its learners is a progressive one.

There are several issues that are currently challenging higher education institutions in South Africa that student service providers have to be cognisant of, and which warrant professionalised responses. Some of these issues have a wider universal applicability, which nevertheless require specialised and equal opportunity policies and practices.

Student diversity: some demographic trends

One of the most dramatic changes in the SA higher education scenario has been the re-composition of the student body. From racially exclusive institutions the current student community on most campuses is rich in diversity extending beyond the consideration of race and gender to include a multiplicity of factors such as:

- ethnicity (language, religion and culture)
- class and privilege
- the impact of differing schooling and learning histories arising from apartheid education
- political affiliation and power struggles among student organizations (SASCO AZASCO, PASO)[10]

- influx of rural students
- students bred in cultures of violence characteristic of present South African society.

One of the consequences of the rapid re-composition of the student population has been the rise of intercultural and interracial tension. Students are divided along racial and ethnic lines, and gender issues constitute a major divisive factor. A cursory glance at the student diaspora on campuses, reveals an interesting territorial separation that is of a voluntary nature. Ironically, although black South Africans fought vigorously for integration and self-determination, they appear now to have wilfully forfeited their right to mix freely with each other. According to Cross (1991), the attention to sociological differences is increasingly valuable, as education becomes more pluralistic in its student population. Multiethnic, multilingual, multiphysical, multiaged and multieconomic and many other heterogeneous labels can be ascribed to a dynamic student population. Cross uses the generic term "new student" to describe the members of a changing population whom she believes have difficulty with main streaming because their values are atypical of the achievement orientation patterns in higher education. The definition of "new student" must undergo constant re-examination to address the new ethnic minority influxes that defy traditional achievement expectations of minorities. Universities' refusal to customise programmes to these populations can result in a new wave of alternate education, thus contributing to unstable enrolment patterns for traditional universities.

This is currently true of the South African tertiary scene where student populations in the historically white institutions are in a constant flux as a result of the competitive efforts of 'varsity colleges' and distance educational institutions whose main attraction lies in their promise of security in homogeneous campuses.

Campus and academic climate

The present scenario at almost every institution of higher learning in the country is one of crisis driven, ad hoc implementation of programmes unassisted by policy or clear procedures. Institutions differ radically in structure, function and reporting lines due to politics and power rather than any clear theoretical frame of reference.

According to Malefo (1996), various factors have been implicated in accounting for achievement outcomes of black students in historically white institutions. These include the level of academic preparation, availability of financial aid, admission requirements, social integration and satisfaction, degree of alienation, perceived supportiveness of the environment and the relative effect of using different adaptational strategies to cope with stressful situations. The degree to which black students perceive their university campuses as being hostile or unsupportive has been a consistent theme in research among Afro-American students in white US institutions (Allen, 1985). Leon (1987) and Honikman (1982) (both cited in Allen, 1985), confirm these findings among South African students. In addition, Prillerman et al (1989) in Louw and Edwards (1993), refers to a 'problematic person environment fit' between black students and the social and academic setting of predominantly white institutions. This in turn has implications for mental health of black students with higher relative vulnerability.

The 'person-environmental fit' is an important factor in establishing effective learning milieu. Staff-student disparities along racial, cultural, and socio-economic levels of privilege are important contributors to the learning climate. While academic staff at the historically white institutions have been raised and nurtured in largely first world environments as members of the former ruling class, their students emerge from third world, first generation victim status. Many, particularly rural cohorts, have never met or socialized with their white lecturers. Their interactions vacillate between extreme passivity to hostile negativity. Few students are comfortable with staff, making role modelling and mentoring difficult. Language spoken in idiom presents a problem from both the perspective of the learner and the educator. A survey conducted at the University of Natal (Rajab, 1991) to assess student perceptions of their university and staff, found race to be a factor in the interface between administration and students. Staff perceptions of students interestingly confirm the prevalence of stereotyping and communication gaps complicated by language and accent difficulties.

While black students experience developmental issues similar to those of other college students, nationally as well as globally, such as adjusting to college, separating from family, developing autonomy, developing career and life plans and realizing educational goals, they may experience these developmental goals differently and more acutely from more advantaged students, given the influence of social, financial and environmental problems.

The establishment of multicultural models of training and development specific to the African context is therefore of importance. This calls for the need for training of existing staff at all tertiary institutions and for the recruitment of new staff with expertise in the area of student services in Southern Africa.

Ethnicity and political trends

The post-apartheid era has brought within its wake a changing political scenario. In the past, university administration at white liberal institutions joined hands with students in protest against government, while this was not the case at Afrikaans-speaking institutions. Today, the scene has changed.

While it was acceptable for liberal white students to criticise the past government, it is not deemed politically correct to do so now. Whereas in the past they had the implicit support of the liberal institutions to do so, they do not anymore. So, freedom of expression and activity has to be seen within the context of changing political climates.

Student discipline

An analysis of student disciplinary statistics reveals a disparity on racial and gender lines, making stereotyping of student groups a natural knee-jerk reaction. Whereas male students are greater offenders by far, the nature of the offences varies along racial lines. Academic integrity issues, such as plagiarism, copying of assignments and during tests, are more prevalent among students whose teaching styles at school levels approximate rote-learning and inculcate bench-bound listening. As passive learners, they are more inclined to plagiarize assignments than their western counterparts. Violent crimes, assault, theft of property, rape are more prevalent among students who are, in the main, products of a traumatic township culture of violence and crime. Such students are in need of therapeutic assistance and remedial attention than harsh punitive measures. However, the realities of an infrastructure that can accommodate an increasing number of such criminal transgressions, is remote.

At a student governance level, the disciplinary issues are mainly around the mismanagement and squandering of funds, a lack of accountability to student constituencies, and undemocratic behaviour in decision-making.

Student conduct and discipline falls directly under the purview of student affairs divisions. Media reports of unruly student behaviour and criminal activities have caused the public to question higher education's ability to control uncivil and/or criminal behaviour and its commitment to traditional moral standards.

Fiscal constraints on programme development

Tertiary institutions (technikons and universities) in South Africa are facing great fiscal problems at the start of the new millennium. With general operating costs rising, an eroded base of financial support, dwindling enrolment especially at the historically disadvantaged institutions, universities are being forced to re-examine how they manage resources. The catchwords, 'Do more with less', 'work smarter not harder' are efforts to streamline a more efficient system. "Downsizing" and "right sizing" have in turn been met with resistance to the opposite calls for affirmative action and equal opportunity. Despite the call for equal opportunity for access to higher education, the reality spells a different picture. Each institution is facing the challenge of reduced funding in unique ways. Some have increased student fees, some have reduced programmes, some have embarked on energy utility, supplies and services conservation plans, but all institutions have been forced to re-examine institutional goals and priorities in the attempt to provide quality programmes and services with a static or reduced fiscal base.

Conclusion

The political and social changes that have swept South Africa in the last ten years have necessitated a re-examination on the part of government, of higher education and its role in nation building, citizenship and employment. Several partnership initiatives are underway, involving civil society, government, business and higher education. The main task of education planners and policy-makers has been to change the education and training system in South Africa bringing it in line with international trends, while synonymously addressing local imperatives. Accordingly, the core values and principles of higher education as advanced in the *Education White Paper 3: A programme for transforming Higher Education 1997* are Equity and Redress, Quality, Development, Effectiveness and Efficiency. The challenge to higher education in South Africa lies in developing a synchronicity between the forces of globalization, international trends and local demands.

In summary, one of the most dramatic changes in the South African higher education system has been the re-composition of the student body in terms of race, culture, gender and past privilege. In stark contrast is the lack of change in the profile of academic staff especially at the historically white institutions. The consequences of this have been a prevalent perception of inadequate role model and mentors. Poor diversity management at most institutions gives rise to inter-cultural and inter racial tensions. The challenge to educationists lies in integrating student populations from historically diverse backgrounds into the system without compromising academic standards. In addition the impact of socio-economic and health issues such as the HIV/AIDS pandemic is an added burden on fiscal demands. The government's Size and Shape Document clearly outlines the necessity to rationalize higher education institutions, preventing unnecessary duplication of resources. Recent problems, like poor fiscal management, low student enrolment numbers, limited financial aid, conflict at senior management level have conspired with inequality, lack of coordination between institutions and course duplication to create an untenable situation.

In addressing the problems of higher education in South Africa, a pragmatic approach is called for, one that encourages synchronicity between all major stakeholders in the higher education.

References

Allen W *Black student, White campus : Structural, interpersonal, and psychological correlates of success.* Journal of Negro Education. 54, 134-147, 1985

Cross, K.P *Beyond the Open Door: New Students to Higher Education.* San Francisco:Jossey-Bass, 1971

Leatt, J V *The Educational Challenges faced by Universities*, April 1992. University of Natal newsletter.

Louw A and Edwards P *Conflicts of interests in Psychology – An Introduction for students in South Africa.* Isando: Lexicon Publishers, 1993

Malefo V M *The effect of family environment, stress and coping behaviours on academic performance among African women students.* University of Natal 1996

Naidoo J *South Africa's rainbow nation, reality or dream?* Laurier Psychology Graduate Newsletter, Spring/Summer Edition, 1998

Rajab D *Interaction patterns of students in tertiary institutions as a function of integration in post-apartheid South Africa.* (Unpublished paper) 1991.

Notes

[1] As recently as 1996, nearly 29% of the population over the age of 19 had received no formal education. 24% had received primary school education.

[2] The education budget now stands at 22% of total government spending (7% of gross domestic budget). Although almost all appropriately aged children are now enrolled in

primary schools, huge education backlogs still frustrate the demands of the job market, besides the rapidly expanding expectations of adult learners whose thwarted educational potential is in need of development.

[3] Getting the equity redistribution in place requires retrenchment of historically advantaged staff and admitting more black staff and eligible students. If universities have as their motto, equity and excellence, they cannot have one without the other.

[4] 'Academics slam proposals to shake up tertiary education institutions'. Report by Edwin Naidu. *Sunday Independent*, 23 July 2000.

[5] The Council on Higher Education has just released a report on The Shape and Size of Higher Education, June 2000. The brief of the task team was to make recommendations towards a transformed rational, seamless, higher education system, responsive to South African's needs and those of the 21st century.

[6] Mamphele Ramphele was, until recently, the first black woman Vice-Chancellor of a historically white institution, the University of Cape Town. A black consciousness advocate, she fought with Steve Biko in the early 1970s.

[7] Naidoo J *South Africa's rainbow nation, reality or dream?* Laurier Psychology Graduate Newsletter, Spring/Summer Edition, 1998.

[8] The budget allocated to each child was determined on a sliding scale by race. The most being spent on the white child and the least on the black child.

[9] Bhengu Mahlengi. Opening address by the chairperson of the National Youth Commission on the occasion of the Summit on National Youth, Braamfontein, Johannesburg. January 1999.

[10] SASCO: South African Students' Congress, AZASCO: Azanian Students' Congress, PASO: Pan African Students' Organization.

Chapter Seven

Disadvantage is complex: targeting special groups is not enough!

Fran Ferrier and Margaret Heagney

Introduction

In Australia the targeting of special groups selected on the basis of particular social and economic characteristics is the primary approach to dealing with inequities in education at all levels. Special plans, programmes, policies and activities are put in place to assist the selected groups to enter, participate and successfully complete formal education in schools, the vocational education and training (VET) sector and higher education.

In this chapter we look at some of the strengths and weaknesses of the target group (equity category) approach and discuss them in the light of our experiences as an equity practitioner and equity researcher over many years. Our comments and arguments draw on the research of the many people (e.g. Clarke *et al* 1997, Dobson *et al* 1998, Eveline 1996, James *et al* 1999) who have contributed to advances in understanding of educational disadvantage in Australia. We also draw on the findings of a project we undertook at Monash University.

In this chapter we do not advocate an end to selecting and targeting particular disadvantaged groups, as there are many reasons to continue the special efforts people in these groups need to be able to access and participate successfully in education. However, we argue that the disadvantage that some people face in entering, participating, completing, and gaining successful outcomes from education is dynamic rather than static, and complex rather than simple and that a focus on target groups by itself is inadequate to address these features.

Target groups in higher education

Student equity in Australian higher education institutions is dominated by federal government policy. Although the national equity blueprint, *A Fair Chance for All* was formulated in

1990, and is thus now more than a decade old, it continues to shape most equity activity.

In *A Fair Chance for All* six groups were identified and designated as disadvantaged on the basis of their under-representation in the higher education student population, compared with their share of the population as a whole. The groups remain the primary focus of equity policies and programmes and are defined in precise operational terms:

- People from socio-economically disadvantaged backgrounds - defined as 'residents in an area with low socio-economic status (SES) as a surrogate for students' low SES'.
- Aboriginal and Torres Strait Islander people - this is a self-nominating group.
- Women in non-traditional areas of study - in which there are less than 40 per cent female enrolments.
- People from non-English-speaking backgrounds, 'those students who were born overseas, arrived in Australia less than 10 years ago and who speak a language other than English at home'.
- People with disabilities - who acknowledge those disabilities at enrolment time and request information on services.
- People from rural and isolated areas - this definition is based on the post code of the students permanent home residence and 'is based on an index of remoteness which combines population density and distance from the nearest provincial city'.

Those familiar with Australian history, will recognise most of these groups as being those traditionally excluded from social, political and economic power.

Monitoring of the performance of the higher education system as whole, and each of the institutions that comprise it, in relation to the target groups, is undertaken through the construction of indicators from data collected annually by the institutions and delivered to the Federal Government. These indicators measure the *access, participation, success* and *retention* of students in the target groups compared with other students. At a national level the information derived from the indicators is used to compare the performance of states and of universities as well as monitoring the progress of the higher education system as a whole towards achieving the equity targets set by the Government. Individual institutions use the indicators to monitor their progress towards the equity targets that they set themselves and to compare their performance with that of similar institutions.

Higher education institutions receiving government funding (which is almost all of the higher education institutions in the country) are required to submit annual equity plans which incorporate their equity data, their equity targets, policies and programmes. Equity plans form part of the educational profiles process – the agreement between government and the universities upon which institutions operating grants are based. Reporting progress against all the target groups is a mandatory requirement of equity plans. However, institutions can choose to place a particular emphasis on some target groups, reflecting local priorities. For instance, in line with the composition of the local population, the Northern Territory University may choose to place a strong emphasis on Aboriginal and Torres Strait Islander students; a university located in an area considered to be socio-economically disadvantaged may choose to make a strong effort to cater for low SES students; a university in a rural city may choose to focus on students from surrounding districts.

Targeting: strengths and weaknesses

Strengths

The target groups approach has proved to be a useful method for dealing with inequity in education for two main reasons. Firstly, it identifies some large groups in society that, in aggregate, suffer substantial levels of measurable educational disadvantage. It focuses the attention of education policy-makers, institutions and practitioners on these groups, and guides the distribution of resources and opportunities toward them. Secondly, the approach enables the performance of educational institutions (and units within them) and systems to be measured and evaluated. Data can be collected for each group and measured over time to indicate progress toward achievement of equity. Knowing that their equity performance will be measured, and that it is linked to (albeit a small amount of) government funding, institutions are encouraged to be pro-active in identifying and addressing the causes and outcomes of disadvantage at the local level.

These strengths of the target group approach have played a part in the achievement of equity gains in education in recent years. For instance the Department of Employment, Training and Youth Affairs (DETYA, 1999) notes that:

- The participation of Indigenous Australians in higher education has increased steadily throughout the 1990s.
- The participation of women in non-traditional fields of study rose in all areas between 1991 and 1997, and women's participation rose also for higher degrees.

- There was a large increase in the participation of students with a disability between 1996 and 1997 (the only two years for which data are available).

However, presenting a counterbalance to the strengths of the target group approach are some weaknesses or drawbacks that have become apparent through experience in using the approach or have been uncovered by research and the development of theory. For instance, the target group concept has been misused for political ends and so has contributed to a growing perception of the groups as 'competing victims' in a contest for limited resources (e.g. Bacchi, 1996). In this way, some groups are cast as more worthy/deserving/needy/undeserving than others, usually based on flimsy or misunderstood data. Equity practitioners may recognise the notion of 'competing victims' in questions such as 'why do we spend so much on *them*?' or 'what about the (some group that is perceived to have missed out)?'

A second weakness of the approach is that it focuses on disadvantage but ignores its counterpart – advantage (Eveline 1996). Treating people within the designated target groups as 'other' points to the existence of a 'norm' - the idea of a typical student -around and for whom educational institutions and systems are constructed. It confines equity considerations perpetually to the margins of educational systems - where they are considered as an 'add on' that can be discarded or downplayed when more important things intervene (e.g. economic circumstances). In contrast, attending also to advantage means asking - and answering- the question, 'who does the system serve?'. This is important because the achievement of equity requires more than the removal of barriers and other difficulties that inhibit access to education and training and work against successful participation and outcomes by some people. Rather it requires a comprehensive examination and possible re-casting of education systems, structures, cultures and practices.

A third weakness of the target group approach is that it tends to stigmatise people within the designated groups. This stigma can compound the disadvantage these students experience, such as by changing the expectations and behaviours of the students and those around them. For instance, some groups of Aboriginal students have complained that they dislike courses that lead to qualifications that are specially designated for them, (e.g. Certificate in office management [Koori]), because in the labour market employers perceive these courses as being of a lower standard (see Ferrier, 1999).

A further drawback of the target group approach is that it has a tendency to be relatively static. The groups recognised in Australian higher education have changed little in ten years. This suggests not only that only limited advances have been made in addressing their needs, but also that there may be only limited recognition of alterations in the particular forms of disadvantage each has experienced during this period. Yet contemporary catch-cries of 'globalisation' and 'technological progress' have in common a theme of rapid change. In the mainstream media, yesterday's and today's worlds are presented as very different, and tomorrow's as beyond our understanding. Substantial changes in social and economic circumstances and political decision-making are likely to have an impact on the patterns of social inclusion and exclusion.

The final and possibly most significant drawback of the target group approach is that it oversimplifies what is in fact a very complex reality. Superficially, each group appears homogeneous and the boundaries between them reasonably robust. However, this is far from the case. There can be many differences in the characteristics and circumstances of individuals or sub-groups counted within the same group (eg.Rural and urban Aboriginal people with very different levels of education and skills). This 'within-group diversity' means that while some similar difficulties (e.g. racism in the case of indigenous students) are experienced, the disadvantage faced by sub-groups and individuals within the one target group may be different in some important respects.

From their research in the Australian Vocational Education and Training system Golding and Volkoff (1999) have noted for instance that

> Not all women, people from non-English speaking backgrounds or rural and isolated people we interviewed were disadvantaged, and not all of those that were disadvantaged were disadvantaged in the same way (p 39).

Statistical studies have shown that many people are counted within more than one equity target group. For instance, a person of low socio-economic status may also be counted as an Aboriginal, of non-English speaking background, from a rural or remote area, and as a woman studying in a non-traditional area. Where such multiple disadvantage occurs research has shown that the problems and barriers that people experience compound to increase the magnitude and impact of the disadvantage. In particular researchers have noted that low socio-economic status is a common central element in the disadvantage experienced by many people in other target groups and makes it harder for them to overcome difficulties that arise, for instance from gender, or rurality (eg Clarke et al 1997, James et al 1999). Analysis of statistics collected by DETYA indicate that in higher education more than 80 percent of low socio- economic status students and 60 percent of rural and isolated students are also counted within other equity groups (Dobson *et al* 1998).

A further complication is that a strong focus on the target groups can lead to a neglect, or masking of disadvantage suffered by people outside these groups - though the barriers and problems these people experience can be substantial. As will be noted later in this chapter, students who are the first in their family to attend university and students with family responsibilities both experience difficulties that impact on their access, participation, success and retention in higher education. Some of these students will be within the designated target groups, others will not.

These weaknesses in the target group approach help to explain some aspects of the poorer equity performance of the higher education system:

- Overall poor rates of success and retention of Indigenous students.
- Continuing low participation rates of people from rural backgrounds.
- Low participation rates of people of low socio-economic status.
- Low participation and retention rates of people from isolated backgrounds.
(DETYA 1999)

The 1999 Monash Equity Project

The complex reality of disadvantage, and the inability of the target group approach to address this reality by itself, was emphasised for us in a small research project we undertook at Monash University in 1999. The research aimed to look beyond the existing target groups to ask are there other forms of disadvantage that the university could and should address. It also sought to clarify how much emphasis the university should continue to put on the target groups in its equity plan, and perhaps, given growing recognition of compound disadvantage, if there were particular groups that should be given a strong focus.

The project was limited in budget and therefore scope. Nevertheless we were able to undertake a number of different research activities, and from them gain insights useful beyond the boundaries of our own institution.

We began by surveying recent Australian literature on emerging student equity issues, then went on to:

- analyse data on the access, participation, success and retention of equity groups at Monash from 1993 to 1999;
- analyse 1999 enrolment data (commencing students and all students);
- draw on a survey of the financial situation of current students, conducted by the Monash Students' Association;
- analyse material provided by applicants for merit-based equity scholarships.

We also consulted students and staff in the university community, including counsellors, community services staff, financial aid and welfare officers, student employment and careers officers, scholarships and student rights staff, students from rural and urban backgrounds, student union staff and office bearers, lecturers and administrators based in faculties on all campuses.

We were asked to undertake this project because Monash University's Student Equity and Access Branch had begun to hear of disturbing anecdotal evidence coming from a variety of sources which indicated there was more to disadvantage than under-representation of students in the six designated equity categories. It included information coming from the university's Exclusions Committees where students rights officers, advocating on behalf of students threatened with exclusion from their courses because of unsatisfactory performance, were reporting a wide range of difficulties encountered by groups of students that did not necessarily relate to the recognised problems of designated equity groups. Among these were students:

- with family responsibilities either as parents, or in relation to extended families;
- working increasingly long hours to gain sufficient financial support and being subject to the demands of employers and irregular shift work;
- who are the first in their family to attend university and thus have a very limited idea of what was required to complete a university course successfully.

Other staff such as academics and administrators in faculties, counsellors and financial aid officers, also identified these groups of students as needing special support. In addition, reports began to surface of some alarming levels of poverty among students unable to afford transport and books and going without meals.

Our examination of equity indicator data showed that overall from 1993-1999 Monash University's performance in relation to the target groups was patchy. Improvements in some measures were offset by declines – or little change- in others. This had occurred in spite of the fact that the university had established a range of initiatives designed to counter recognised disadvantage:

- With the exception of people with disabilities access for all target groups was lower in 1999 than in 1993. Access for Aboriginal students showed particular volatility.

- Participation showed improvements for people with disabilities, younger people from low SES backgrounds and people from non-English speaking backgrounds, but declined for all other groups. Participation for Aboriginal students showed the same pattern as access. Rural students and low SES remain the most under-represented of all the groups.

- Success rates are generally high across most groups and have fluctuated very little. Declines are noted in the cases of Aboriginal and Isolated students.

- Apparent retention rates indicated particular problems in the case of Aboriginal and isolated students.

Analysis of enrolment data confirmed the existence of complex patterns of within group diversity and multiple or compound disadvantage. It showed that among *low SES* students, for instance, are mature age and young students, students enrolled part-time, full-time and externally, Aboriginal and non-Aboriginal students, female and male students, urban and rural students, etc. It also showed a particular overlap of students in the groups *Aboriginal, low SES and rural and isolated.* The data suggested that the lack of success in achieving improvement in the access, participation, success and retention of the target groups might reflect the complex and compound nature of the disadvantage students were experiencing.

The material we collected in consultations and from the student financial survey and equity scholarship applications provided confirmation that particular disadvantage was being experienced by students with family responsibilities, students trying to combine work and study, and students who were the first in their family to attend university. It indicated also that this disadvantage was particularly marked where a student experienced more than one of these problems. Sometimes circumstances changed rapidly so that a student who had planned carefully to balance commitments was left in unexpected but considerable difficulties.

Students experiencing difficulties because of family responsibilities were not only those with children, but also students caring for siblings, elderly parents or other relatives. In addition to regular and ongoing difficulties (e.g. lack of affordable childcare), from time to time these students also had unexpected commitments that could not be abrogated, but which impacted legitimately on their ability to participate in their study and to meet assessment and other deadlines. (For instance, a student might be called on to translate for non-English speaking family members in a medical emergency.) Students expressed concerns about the lack of understanding of their difficulties that was manifest in refusals by staff to consider that caring for sick children, parents or grandparents was considered a sufficient reason to grant an extensions of time to complete an assignment.

The material we collected indicated that for students who are the first in their family to attend university a lack of understanding among their family and friends, together with their own misconceptions about what is involved in university study, can create pressures and difficulties that threaten their retention and ultimate success. In particular we learned of non English-speaking-background students and/or low SES students, who are also the first in their family to attend university and who can also be under pressure to work long hours in family businesses, particularly in the case of an illness in the family.

The material told of surprisingly high numbers of students suffering severe financial difficulties that were affecting their participation in a variety of ways. There were students going without food and thus losing concentration and becoming open to illness; homeless students without a place to study or rest, including some living in their cars; students unable to afford essential transport to attend class or use the library or other resources; students suffering the upheaval of having to move to cheaper accommodation.

These students were not necessarily from low SES backgrounds. For instance, they included a group of young students nominally considered to be from a medium or high SES background and studying at a Monash campus located in a summer tourist destination. Though provided with accommodation by their families (often in the form of the family holiday house) they had no money for living or study expenses and because of their parents' high income were ineligible for government support. Part-time work opportunities in the area were also scarce. These students had come to light when they sought emergency grants to pay for food and books.

We learned that earning the money they need to live even at a very basic level creates difficulties for students in combining this work with their study. To make matters worse, these difficulties have been compounded by a changing industrial relations climate which has enabled employers to demand and expect flexibility. Workers are expected to meet irregular hours, sometimes at short notice.

Discussion

Our analysis of the equity indicator data for Monash University found that the focus of equity effort on the DETYA groups has produced the same sort of mixed results for these groups as have been achieved for the higher education system as a whole. That is, slow and small progress in some cases has been matched by little or even backward movement in others. In particular, access and participation for rural and low socio-economic background students remain problematic, as do the success and retention of Aboriginal and Torres Strait Islander students. Not discussed here but also of note were variations in the results from one campus of Monash University to another. These bore similarities to variations in results for different universities within the higher education system and can be related to differences in the goals, locations, culture, course offerings and student catchment of each campus, as well as to the success of some equity initiatives at the local level.

Given the focus of attention on the DETYA equity groups, why has progress been so limited? Some clues emerge from other findings of our research. Our analysis of enrolment data found that the groups are far from homogeneous, with members of the same group coming from a variety of different socio-economic, cultural and educational backgrounds. Yet a tendency to assume homogeneity has underlain ongoing work in all educational sectors to identify and address the specific causes and experiences of disadvantage for each group. Though important work that has been useful in guiding equity initiatives, this may have had the unintended consequence of over-simplifying the picture of disadvantage experienced by these groups and led to simplistic solutions being applied to what may be very complex problems.

Secondly, enrolment data show an overlap in the groups, particularly rural, low socio-economic background and Aboriginal and Torres Strait Islander students. This overlap leads to the conclusion that some students experience more than one type of disadvantage. As we noted earlier, recent equity research has indicated that where this occurs, the disadvantage these students experience has been found to compound so that it becomes stronger and more difficult to counter.

Further, the superficial simplicity of disadvantage implied by the group approach is not borne out in the picture of disadvantage that emerges from material we collected through consultations and from surveys and scholarship applications. This picture indicates disadvantage to be complex rather than simple and dynamic rather than static. That is, it is multi-dimensional and can change rapidly and substantially. It also shows that considerable disadvantage can be experienced by students outside the equity groups - such as students with work or family responsibilities and students who lack understanding of what is involved in study at the university level, such as those who are the first in their family to participate in higher education.

Putting together the results of our research with the findings of previous equity researchers leads to an understanding of disadvantage that is far removed from the notion of under-representation on which the selection of the DETYA equity groups was based. In this view, some students will experience disadvantage that relates to characteristics they share with others. For instance, though they may differ in socio-economic or educational background and geographical location, many Aboriginal and Torres Strait Islander students will suffer in similar ways from racism or cultural misunderstandings. Similarly, people whose first language is not English may experience similar difficulties in spite of varying backgrounds. This understanding has guided considerably equity effort to date and remains the major strength of the group approach. In addition though, the research has allowed us to see that the particular forms of disadvantage that each person experiences can be highly individualised as the individual's particular circumstances (which may alter from time to time) interact or clash with inflexibility in the policies, activities, rules and regulations of the universities and the understandings of their staff.

For instance, the inflexible timetabling of a course may not pose an initial difficulty for students who must also work for financial support if they can arrange working hours and other commitments to suit. But inflexibility will create a problem if an employer decides to demand a non-negotiable change in working hours, or sudden and unexpected family commitments arise. A strict assessment policy may become more problematic where a student is affected by an illness in the family that requires the fulfilment of temporary family responsibilities. A sudden and unexpected loss of employment may cause a sudden decline in a student's income that puts beyond the student's reach the purchase of required books or travel to, or between, campuses.

This understanding of disadvantage (which we call *dynamic disadvantage*) places a focus not so much on individuals, or even groups of individuals, but on the structures, rules, regulations, practices and policies of higher education institutions and the understandings which underpin the ways in which these are applied by their staff. It thus supports a shift in the current direction of much equity effort.

Implications for equity planning

Article 26 of the Universal Declaration of Human Rights states that 'everyone has the right to education' and 'higher education shall be equally accessible to all on the basis of merit'. Moreover, there is no evidence that academic ability differs by race, class, gender, or address. Though ten years of effort has now gone into seeking *A Fair Chance For All*, equity continues to be elusive in the higher education system. What can be done to speed progress?

Being complex and dynamic in nature, disadvantage is very unlikely to be addressed successfully by simple, short-term strategies. A successful response will be sustained, multi-faceted and able to accommodate and adapt to change. It will incorporate initiatives at both the local levels(faculty/campus/university) and the systemic level (across institutions).

An important consideration when looking at options is that the capacity of the universities to act to achieve sustainable change is limited. By themselves, universities cannot redress the many problems that arise from the social, economic, political and educational disparities that characterise our communities. The universities, for instance, cannot solve the problems of poverty that force people into work rather than study, or combinations of the two. At best they can expose these problems, lobby governments and provide some short-term assistance to students suffering from related difficulties. However, it is well within the capacity of the institutions to alter those things about themselves that create or heighten the difficulties that students, or potential students, experience.

The limited success and continuing problems demonstrated at both the systemic and institutional levels by the equity indicators indicate that continued attention to the particular needs of people in the DETYA equity groups is warranted. However, given what we now know about disadvantage, we must take greater care not to underestimate the complexity of the disadvantaged experienced by people in these groups. We must make an effort to ensure we do not assume that all people in one equity group are the same and face similar difficulties.

We must also ensure we do not forget that the difficulties they experience can compound each other. This might require some innovative and creative responses at the local level and working more closely with these people to meet their changing needs. We must also take care not to contribute to the political misuse of the groups as 'competing victims' or to the stigmatisation of people within these groups. In addition we must also remain open to the possibility that in new times, new groups may be emerging that will require our attention. These groups may differ at the local and systemic levels and their identification may not necessarily start from the basis of under-representation in the student population.

Most importantly though, we must pay more attention to factors in the structures and operations of our higher education system and its institutions that create and sustain disadvantage. This will mean increasing efforts to centralise equity and to move it forward from its present marginal position. This will involve countering the notion of a norm or 'typical' student that has tended to underlie and reinforce rules, regulations and policies. It will also mean facing up to the dominance of particular cultural understandings that contribute to this inflexibility and thus to disadvantage.

Conclusion

Target groups continue to provide a useful framework for addressing many equity issues in higher education institutions. However, disadvantage presents in different ways in different situations. Equity efforts need to take into consideration the myriad manifestations and complex patterns of disadvantage and the ways in which they can change. By itself, the target-group approach is not enough to do this. In order to respond to the issues around student equity and disadvantage such as those thrown up by our study, it is necessary to consider options which take account of multiple and dynamic disadvantage while trying to avoid the pitfalls of conventional approaches.

Based on new understandings of disadvantage we suggest moving away from existing approaches and increasingly attempting to make equity more central (and therefore less marginal) to the operations of the institution. We advocate that flexibility be implemented on a broad scale throughout the institution. This can be combined with ongoing provision of a range of targeted student support services. We also recommend exposing and interrogating the norm of a 'typical' student and its role in institutional policies and practices.

Our work demonstrates the importance of being flexible when dealing with the complexities of disadvantage, of constant monitoring and reviewing equity strategies, so that they deal with the reality of students' disadvantage not historical constructions of it.

References

Bacchi, C. L. (1996) *The politics of affirmative action: women, equality and category politics,* Sage Publications, London.

Butler, E. and Ferrier, F. (1999) *Don't be too polite girls! Women, work and VET, a critical review of the literature,* NCVER Adelaide.

Clarke, J. Zimmer, B. and Main, R. (1997) Under-representation in Australian higher education by the socio-economically disadvantaged: review of trends and issues and implications for university planning and practice. Paper presented at the Australasian Association for Institutional Research (AAIR), 8th International Conference. Adelaide, and 26-28 November.

Department of Employment, Education and Training (1990) *A Fair Chance for All: higher education that's within everyone's reach.* Australian Government Publishing Service, Canberra.

Department of Education, Training and Youth Affairs (1999) Equity in higher education, Occasional Paper 99A, Higher Education Division, Canberra.

Department of Education, Training and Youth Affairs (1997) *Selected Higher Education Student Statistics, Preliminary,* Australian Government Publishing Service, Canberra.

Dobson, I. Sharma, R. and Ramsay, E. (1998) Designated equity groups in Australian universities: performance of commencing undergraduates in selected course types, Australian Vice-Chancellors' Committee, Canberra.

Eveline, Joan. (1994) The Politics of Advantage in *Australian Feminist Studies, Autumn* 1994, pp 129-154.

Ferrier, F. (1999) in Ferrier F and Anderson, D (eds), *Different drums - one beat? Economic and social goals in education and training,* NCVER, Adelaide.

Golding, B. and Volkoff, V. (1999) *Creating outcomes: individuals and groups on the VET journey,* Centre for the Study of Higher Education, University of Melbourne.

James, R. Wyn, J. Baldwin, G. Hepworth, G. McInnis, C. and Stephanou, A. (1999) Rural and isolated school students and their higher education choices, NBEET, AGPS, Canberra.

Universal Declaration of Human Rights (1948) G.A. res 217A(III), U.N.Doc A/810 at 71

Chapter Eight

Tuition fees: policy, theory and realities of access to higher education in the UK

Julie Ann Andreshak

Introduction

In 1997, following the recommendations of the Dearing Report (the report of The National Committee of Inquiry into Higher Education, 1997), the British government announced its decision to enact a tuition scheme for undergraduate university students. The introduction of a tuition fee, initially up to a maximum of £1000 per year for first-degree post-secondary students, hardly came as a surprise; nonetheless, it was and is a topic of much debate in academia and the popular press. The reform implemented by government (which was somewhat different than the recommendations of Report) constitutes a plan to:

- charge students an up-front tuition fee that will be 'means-tested' (based on their ability to pay);
- increase the availability of student loans by that amount;
- eliminate all remaining grants for maintenance (living expenses), switching exclusively to means-tested (need-based) loans.

This reform came after a series of measures taken since the 1980s to reduce the percentage of public funding used for higher education in Britain. The increasing rate at which private monies (either corporate or personal) are contributing to tertiary education is by no means unique to Britain. In fact, this policy is representative of a worldwide trend to shift higher education from a public good to a private one, creating markets (or 'quasi-markets') through which educational systems are funded.

The locus of control, once seen as firmly in the grips of the state and the academy, has shifted toward the market in at least three critical ways. First, government has reduced research funding to institutions and increased control over public funds granted. Second, the state has advised universities to become more entrepreneurial and seek out corporate and philanthropic money, thus ceding some control over research to the donors. Third, students and their families must contribute towards higher education courses, making them consumers and thus forcing schools to compete for student funds.

The purpose of this chapter is to briefly examine the tuition-fees policy through three different, but interrelated, lenses. The widest lens envisions how this policy is a piece of a larger political, social, and economic change; the second reveals the theoretical, philosophical, and empirical backing of the reform; and, the third lens looks at the policy from the perspective of ethical merit; that is, what are the potential impacts, if any, of the policy on access to higher education for underrepresented groups, particularly lower social classes.

Context

The big picture

The relationship between higher education, government, industry, and the public is rapidly changing. Massification of higher education in both less-developed nations and more-developed nations has put considerable strain on university resources. Moreover, as government and industry aspire to "high-tech" economies, the research and workers needed to produce such an economy need to be reshaped. These changes require re-examining how universities are funded, who should attend university, what roles the university ought to play, who is accountable to whom and by what means this accountability should manifest itself, and, most fundamentally, what the purpose of higher education institutions is. In Britain, this is certainly the case.

While Cambridge and Oxford still remain at the pinnacle of higher education in Britain, the days of the university as totally independent institutions (financially and otherwise) are long gone. By the end of World War I, the military and technology needs of Britain were seen in a new light with university research as the flagship of such advancements. Additionally, war veterans returned with the desire to attend university (Bligh, 1990, 32). This expansion required the government to begin helping to pay the costs of both teaching and research. Nonetheless, the amount of research money granted to universities remained small, and student enrolments still represented an elite segment of the population.

Gradually, funding from government for university research increased, and the University Grants Committee was established for the purpose of distributing government money for university research purposes, and in doing so creating a 'buffer' between government partisan pressures and academic integrity. A different tone began to be reflected in the approach toward funding students, as well. In 1963, the highly influential Robbins Report was published and what became to be known as the 'Robbins principle' was accepted:

> This stated that places in higher education should be provided for all of those qualifying for entry ... the [Robbins] Committee ... based its recommendation not only on the political concept of a citizenship right to higher education (for the qualified) but also on economics and sociology: the need for national investment to match that of Britain's national competitors, and the expectation that expansion would lead to a less socially-skewed pattern of participation (Fulton, 1991, 589).

Acting on this rationale, student fees were paid by the national government to the local government which then furnished the universities with fees that covered about 10% of teaching costs. Students were given grants to cover living expenses.

By the 1980s, however, Britain had moved toward a massified system. This has made higher education an 'expectation, not just an opportunity, for the children, of both sexes, of upper middle-class families,' but a system where "the proportion of working-class students was falling" (italics added) (Fulton, 1991, 594). Hence, while 'mass' in number, an equitable distribution of students from all socio-economic (SES) groups was not yet a reality.

In order to encourage schools to increase enrolments, the government increased its contribution to 30% of teaching costs per student during the next decade. By 1994, the increase in numbers was so large that, despite the fact that per student costs were decreasing, the government could not afford to continue funding at this level (Williams, 1998, 78). This being the case, the British government needed to begin seeking other ways in which to fund higher education.

Hence, the notion of public funding of higher education necessarily took an ideological turn. The last decade of the twentieth century gave way to the erosion of the student grant system and the abolition of the University Grants Committee.

Student tuition fees: enter Dearing

The issue of student-fees is central to the notion that the locus of control is moving away from state planning and control and into the hands of the "consumer." In yet another move in the direction of the market, there is question as to whether or not students (like industry or government in the case of research) are the best and most capable decision makers. In theory, if student places in various disciplines are allocated via central planning the needs of economy can be met.

This is most easily accomplished by disallowing consumer choice by government funding of places in higher education, in particular supporting disciplines that it deems necessary for the national interest. 'Externalities' (economic growth, new knowledge, political participation) impact the society and therefore deem government control necessary and desirable (Eicher & Chevaillier, 1991, 95). On the other hand, Eicher and Chevaillier (1991) also point out that the notion of 'student as consumer' can be valuable in that a social service or public good is not used efficiently or valued by the consumer if it is free (95).

This theoretical debate, when applied to Britain's higher education system, began to lean heavily toward the side of market mechanisms. Beginning in 1988, the Conservative Government of Margaret Thatcher altered public spending in the areas of health care, housing, and education, attacking the 'welfare state' and replacing it with market or market-like structures (Le Grand, 1991, 1257). Ironically, the tuition reform was not actually adopted until Tony Blair's Labour Party came into office in 1997.

This was Thatcher's answer to the mass system created by the end of the twentieth century which could no longer be supported solely by government money. The increase in the numbers of students participating in higher education reached 30% of the 18-year-old cohort by the mid 1990s (Shattock, 1994). Therefore, in 1995, student numbers were capped and spending fell (in real terms) (Barr, 1997, 31). In response, universities threatened to begin charging 'top-up fees' to make up the difference in the loss of funding from government. With the higher education system in turmoil, the Dearing Committee was commissioned with the task of defining British higher education for the next twenty years.

Just as the Robbins Report of the 1960s was in part a response to a decline in British power following the Second World War and the industrial age, the Dearing Report is a response to the era of globalization in which "the state . . . is placing new demands on higher education to lead the competitive struggle in the new post-industrial society" (Mauch & Sabloff, 1995, XV).

Analysing the reform

Theoretical foundations

According to Williams (1992), the desirability of furthering a market-orientation in higher education can be reduced to three main principles: '(1) the belief that the private sector can relieve governments of some of the cost burden; (2) because many of the benefits of higher education accrue to private individuals, the latter should be prepared to pay for them; (3) both the external and internal efficiencies of institutions improve if government agencies operate a social market by buying services from universities and colleges rather than making grants to them' (67).

In relation to principle number one, quite simply, if students and their families are responsible for partly funding their education, it will cost the government less. However, only if *private banks* (and not government) are loaning money to students is the government any better off. Otherwise, the scheme will offer no savings to the government in the short-term. Currently, the loan scheme is public both in its administration and as the source of funds. Therefore, the loans are still causing the problem of undesired public funding. It is projected that it will be twenty-five years before the government will see gains, unless the current debt owned by the government is sold to private banks and future loans are granted by private sources (Barr, 1997).

Second, the ideological principle of higher education as a *private* good is used to bolster the rationale of the reform. This position slices off a section of human capital theory which espouses that an educated population is a population that can contribute to the economy and economic development *along with* improving the lives of the individuals themselves (Fagerlind & Saha, 1989, 18). However, unlike primary and secondary education, the returns from higher education most strongly impact on the income of the individual.

In addition, Fagerlind and Saha (1989) note that education is connected with citizenship and "has been regarded ... as the main agent for the political socialisation of the young into the political culture and ... the main contributor to political integration and the building of national political consciousness" (1989, 125). Whereas the Robbins Report of 1963 used this rationale to firm up the position of heavily subsidizing higher education for any student who qualified and wished to attend, thirty years later Glennerster (1991), puts forth the argument that these issues do *not* apply to tertiary education and that "the aim of public policy is to ensure that individuals invest optimally in *their own human capital* and have the resources to do so. The citizenship goals that attach to community schooling become irrelevant as young people move away from home (1273 'italics added') (See also Friedman, 1962). Likewise, according to Dearing (1997)

...The evidence of measurable benefits from higher education shows that graduates are certainly the major beneficiaries. (There is) a strong link – in aggregate – between participation in full-time undergraduate education and the relative subsequent earnings potential of an individual . . . those with higher education qualifications have higher employment rates, enjoy higher salaries (and) enjoy an average private return of some 11 to 14 percent (para 18.13).

While this may be true, the graduates that are earning more are often *themselves* children of graduates (Wagner, 1995). Thus, the issue of 'cultural capital' arises in that those of better means are often the ones most able to access and ascertain those services. Educated parents are at an advantage in that 'higher political efficacy and greater access to, and better understanding of, culture, science and technology' provide them the knowledge to navigate the system (Eicher & Chevaillier, 1991, 95).

It has also been theorized that government subsidies through tuition payments and grants help those in *higher* socio-economic classes, not those most in need (i.e. they are *regressive* measures). Since most university students come from higher-income families and find higher-paid jobs upon graduation, those most able to pay are receiving their education at the expense of the public (Le Grand, 1991, 1261). Hence, given the low participation rate among those in the lowest socio-economic classes, these families indirectly pay for services they do not use, and at a higher rate (taken against income) (Williams, 1998, 82). Likewise, without differential payments in accordance with real cost, more expensive programs and/or more prestigious universities (Oxbridge or top London schools) often lead to higher salaries (Horn, 1997, 19). Hence, students who have greater access (through a privileged upbringing and greater cultural capital) and who will earn more upon graduation actually are contributing *less* in real terms.

In turn, if the universities calling for top-up fees (e.g. Oxbridge) are allowed to charge these additional fees, the inaccessibility of such institutions will be that much greater for those without the means to pay. On the other hand, if the schools are *not* allowed to charge them, they will be in a position to recruit *more* international students (since they are now required to pay full fees).

The third tenet to the theory is that of economic competition. Although Williams (1992) only makes mention of 'government agencies' as consumers, the same theory can be applied to individual students. With some reference to the American model, it is hypothesized that if students are tuition payers, they will act (and be treated as) as consumers. These 'consumers' of university education will force universities to offer what it is that students want and will fail to survive if they cannot. Undergraduate teaching, then, will prosper as a result of this competition since students' money (a.k.a. loans) will drive quality and efficiency. ' . . . economic efficiency is served if individuals pay directly for services that they receive, and that the high rates of taxation needed to provide them out of public funds are a barrier to wider economic efficiency' (Williams, 1998, 82).

From an equity point of view, the proper choice of pay-back schemes could deal effectively with some equity problems. Income-contingent repayments (such as is currently the case in Britain [excluding Scotland]), for instance, minimize the 'risk' to the student thus presenting a more encouraging picture for members of lower SES groups (Barr, 1993, 721). Mortgage-type loans, (which are not income-contingent, e.g. in the United States) on the other hand, are more likely to scare away students from lower income families since they are assuming debt without the absolute assurance of future income. A 'graduate tax' is yet another repayment possibility. With the graduate tax, graduates are taxed a given percentage each year according to income. Williams (1998) states that therefore students would end up paying more or paying less than the sum that they would have had they borrowed. He further comments that it is difficult to assess who would be required to pay the tax, i.e. what constitutes a degree, what about students who do not complete their studies, and would the tax be paid according to number of years of higher education received? (83).

Empirical Evidence

To assess the validity of a user-fee versus government grant scheme is to assess the degree to which the policy can meet its goals to:

1) relieve government of some financial burden
2) distribute payment of services to those who benefit from said services
3) increase efficiency
4) increase/maintain quality
5) widen access.

Due to the newness of this reform, the empirical evidence has yet to be fully illuminated. However, evidence from similar circumstances can be used to provide a certain amount of validity to the theoretical claims above.

Statistically, those with university degrees do earn more. However, Barr (1993) indicates, "post-primary education is associated with increased productivity, *but does not cause it*" (719). He goes on to note that:

> Though belief in the external benefits of education is widespread, again measurement problems make definitive answers impossible. The heart of the difficulty is the inability to measure the tendency for the education of individual A to increase B's productivity. Estimates of private rates of return are suspect because, of necessity, they omit non-monetary returns such as job satisfaction (719).

Second, the notions of efficiency and access in an essentially market-driven system are validated through the United States higher education system. This is a highly diversified system, with a wide range of post-secondary options. Technical/vocational schools, community colleges, liberal arts colleges, and research universities, have different aims and offer different programmes to cater to the diverse needs of 40% of the 18-year-old cohort (the largest percentage of participation of any nation) enrolled in higher education. Thus, the American market serves the population well in terms of access and (external) efficiency.

However, Trow (1981) indicates that this comparison between the British and American systems in this regard is not without problems. The British system has historically prided itself on high standards for admission and high quality study, resulting in narrow access. On the other hand, wide access in the United States has had the consequence of devaluing the university credential (i.e. the return rate to the individual decreases) and quality (following the lower standards for secondary education) is sacrificed as evidenced by remedial courses at the university level (Trow, 1981, 104-105)

upper awards. It was interesting ʃo note that a high proportion of the Black African group are being awarded Third class honours (11.3%), Intermediate awards (9.6%) and Unclassified degrees (4.3%) instead.

Table 7: Final qualification by ethnic origin: First degree students only

	White	Black African	Black Caribbean	Indian	Chinese	Pakistani Bangladeshi
First Class Honours	12.1	0.9	2.1	5.2	6.8	5.1
Upper Second Honours	49.6	17.4	36.1	38.7	52.3	36.4
Third Class Honours	2.2	11.3	9.3	2.3	4.5	4.0
Unclassified Degree	1.7	4.3	2.1	0.6	0.0	2.0
Intermediate Award	3.5	9.6	2.1	5.8	4.5	6.1
Total	895	115	97	173	44	99

What is important to consider is that given their entry qualifications, the degree outcomes between the ethnic groups perhaps ought to have been different. Students of white origin, for instance, received higher awards than one would have predicted given their entry qualifications. Surprisingly, Indian, Bangladeshi and Pakistani students achieved lower degree awards than their white counterparts, despite having, on average, higher entry qualifications. The outcomes for the Black African group was partly consistent with their average lower entry qualifications, but it did not appear to explain their degree performances to a sufficient extent. It would be difficult to ascertain exactly what is happening to Black African students between the period of arrival and the time of graduation without a larger data set spread over a number of years.

Examination of degree achievements across the different socio-economic groups revealed that around 80% of students from higher social class backgrounds (manager and professional occupational backgrounds) obtained upper and lower second class degrees compared to around 70% of students in the lower social class groups. Students coming from 'sales occupation' backgrounds appeared to perform relatively poorly in their degrees compared to their peers, with higher proportions of the lower social class group achieving third class and intermediate degrees.

Given that the pre-entry qualifications of the lower social groups were almost similar to the higher social class groups (with the exception of the 'sales occupation' group) it could not be used to explain why differences transpired in final degree performances among the social class groups. However, as the figures for the social class sample were small in this sample, we would need to be cautious about the inferences we make from this data.

Finally, analysis of age and degree performance revealed that age was a significant factor in predicting degree performances with 80% of younger students (aged below 24) likely to achieve second class degrees compared to around 70% of students aged 25 and over. Mature students appeared to be more likely to be awarded thirds in their degrees.

3. Conclusion

The analysis of graduates leaving this inner-city university in 1997 presented a complex picture. There were differences between ethnic, social class, gender and age groups in many of the areas looked at, although a major problem was that some of the differences between ethnic groups were based on small numbers.

A summary of some of the preliminary findings were:

1. There have been improvements in the participation rates of ethnic groups, but not so much in relation to social class groups.
2. Unequal distribution and under-representation does not only exist for the lower social class groups; it is also manifest among the sex groups within particular minority ethnic groups. Under representation of Black Caribbean males and Bangladeshi females maybe of particular concern.
3. Differences between social class and minority ethnic groups in terms of final degree performance do not appear to be easily explained, even if we take into account pre-entry qualifications.
4. Age proved to be an important differentiating factor between ethnic groups, with higher proportions of mature students (aged 31 and above) among Black African, Caribbean and Chinese students, respectively. As age also appeared to be related to degree

performances (with mature students less likely to achieve upper class degree) this may have important implications for universities.

The findings examining retention rates within social class and ethnic groups were also useful because there appeared to be some indication that there were differences in drop-out rates (from studies) between the lower and higher social class groups, and between the Black African group and other minority ethnic groups. Unfortunately due to extremely small cell sizes we need to be cautious about the findings. Perhaps what may be required is more extensive measurement of retention (or non-continuation rates) by particular social, ethnic and gender groups in order to identify the extent of the problem. What may also be required is to look at why people from particular groups may be withdrawing from their studies.

This research clearly indicates that there are several reasons why many universities cannot assume that they are currently meeting the needs of their entrants to a satisfactory extent. Examination of degree performance, for instance, revealed that black and (some) Asian students appeared to be disadvantaged just as 'working class' students: on average, these groups performed less well than other students within this inner-city university. But it was also clear that universities would benefit enormously from moving beyond superficial examinations, and being more precise about which of these groups of students were disadvantaged; this study clearly demonstrated that there was substantial within-group diversity among the minority ethnic groups. In addition, the ethnic and social class differences in degree outcomes (even after taking into account pre-entry qualifications) as well as differentials in retention rates within the study indicated that this inner-city university was also failing to recognise (let alone meet) the nature of the distinctive needs of different groups.

Although this was a small research study, it clearly highlights the point that higher education institutions can substantially benefit from research that helps them to *understand* why particular groups are disadvantaged, and furthermore, to understand in such a way that they can find ways of overcoming these disadvantages. Overall, it appears that higher education institutions may have the same problem as researchers in the sixties (examining secondary school achievement) had in relation to social class; the latter has not been mitigated, but now in addition, we have groups in further and higher education whose disadvantages are also somehow related to their ethnicity. What we do have now, however, are a wider range of both theoretical ideas on which to draw on as well as research methods which we can use. This kind of research could do a great deal to illuminate the problems of why universities are currently failing in their provision.

References

Craft, M. and Craft, A. (1983) The participation of ethnic minorities in further and higher education. *Educational Research* 25,1, 10-19.

Drew, D. and Gray, J. (1990) The fifth year examination achievements of black young people in England and Wales. *Educational Research* 32,1, 107-117.

Haque, Z. (2000) The Ethnic Minority Underachieving Group? Investigating the claims of 'underachievement' amongst Bangladeshi pupils in British secondary schools. *Race, Ethnicity and Education*, 3, 2, 145-168.

Kely, T. (1996) Access and equity From Continuing Education to Lifelong Learning: A review of UACE Strategy and Objectives, *Occasional paper, 20*.

Lyon, E.S. (1988) Unequal opportunities: black minorities and access to higher education. *Journal of Further and Higher Education*, 12, 3, 21-37.

Modood, T., Berthoud and others(1997) Ethnic Minorities in Britain: Diversity and Disadvantaged. *The Fourth National Survey of Ethnic Minorities*. London: Policy Studies Institute.

Modood, T. and Acland, T (1998) *Race and higher education*. London: Policy Studies Institute.

Nuttall, D.L., Goldstein, H., Prosser, R. and Rasbath, J. (1989) Differential school effectiveness *International Journal of Educational Research* 13, pp. 769-76.

Skellington, R. and Moriss, P. (1992) *Race in Britain Today*. London, Sage.

Smith, D.J. and Tomlinson, S. (1989) *The School Effect: A Study of Multiracial Comprehensives*. London: Policy Studies Institute.

Swann Report - Cmnd 9453 (1985) *Education for All: Final Report of the Committee of the Inquiry into the Education of Children from Ethnic Minority Groups*. London, HMSO.

Troyna, B. (1984) Fact or Artefact? The "educational underachievement" of black pupils *British Journal of Sociology of Education* 5, 2, pp.153-166.

Note

[1] This is the same as the data that is compiled for the Higher Education Statistics Agency (HESA).

[2] It should also be noted that the sample size varies according to different variables looked at as there are missing values attached to every variable.

[3] Social class is derived from a request on the UCAS (Universities and Colleges Admission Service) application form for the applicant to provide the occupation of the parent, step-parent or guardian with the highest income in the household
[4] There was a very large group students categorised in the 'unknown category'
[5] Based on the age of students when they graduated.

Chapter Ten

African American access to higher education through sports: fulfilling a dream or perpetuating a stereotype?

Judith Brooks-Buck and Eugene L. Anderson

Introduction

...the blind faith of black youths and their families in sport as the prime vehicle of self-realization and social-economic advancement, have combined to generate a complex of critical problems for black society. At the root of these problems is the fact that black families have been inclined to push their children toward sports-career aspirations, often to the neglect and detriment of other critically important areas of personal and cultural development. (Edwards, 1999: p.1).

This chapter attempts to provide an overview of African American access to higher education through sports, and the intended and unintended consequences that result from leaving college without earning a degree. It adds a new dimension to the discourse that has as its foci, the worth of collegiate athletic competition to the athlete and the university. Furthermore, the chapter suggests that many of those who have gained instant fortunes realise the limited parameters of athletic prowess, and the need for more substantive skill development.

Athletic access to higher education

Athletic scholarships, for those who would never be able to afford the luxury of academic preparation, have become the method used most by prominent universities to allow African American students to play in the National Collegiate Athletic Association (NCAA) Division I Sports. The NCAA is the governing body for collegiate athletics. Founded in 1906, the NCAA includes 964 schools classified in three divisions. The size, membership fees, entrance requirements and other standards are applied when determining membership levels. Athletes in Division I compete at the highest collegiate level. The NCAA sponsors 81 championships in 22 sports with almost 24,500 men and women student athletes. However, football and basketball continue to hold the promise of millions of dollars for winners and losers and the universities they represent. Membership in the NCAA is voluntary and of course, has its privileges (Cobb, 1995; Dempsey, 1999).

Moving from hopelessness to hope, young athletes leave home regularly to attend large universities with unlimited resources. Many of these students hope to gain national exposure that will provide an avenue into a lucrative career in professional sports. In reality, of the 1,000,000 high school athletes participating in top level (or varsity) sports each year, fewer than 150 make it to the rank of professional football player. Only three percent of this group will play professional sports for more than one year. The rate for basketball players is even lower, with one in 10,000 making the transition from high school athlete to professional sports figure (Dempsey, 1999).

African Americans comprise 85% of those who are selected to play professional basketball, and 75% of those selected to play professionally in America's National Football League (Cobb, 1995). While in high school, these athletes are doggedly recruited, and provided with a virtual cornucopia of options. Parents are promised that at the end of a college career, a scholar and athlete will be properly prepared for entrance into society. Unfortunately for most, the former option is never realized, and one injury may serve to exclude the latter goal as well. To the student athlete, the dream of becoming a professional may far outweigh the parental dream of earning a college degree (Edwards, 1994; Wilbon, 1997). In actuality, too few athletes earn a degree. Significant obstacles are seen as causal factors.

Student athletes usually have five years of eligibility for sports and six years to complete a degree (typically earned in four years by non-athletes). If one receives a scholarship for athletics that does not last throughout the entire collegiate experience, failure to earn a degree is the usual result. This factor alone is disconcerting for those concerned with the issue of low graduation rates for student athletes. Graduation rates for all Division I student athletes ranged from 52% in 1984 to 58% in 1992. Graduation rates for African American students in the same universities ranged from 33% to 40% respectively, during the same period (1998 NCAA Graduation Rate Summary). Additionally, for those who decide to play for Division I universities, sports activities regularly consume large amounts of study and class time. For example, in September 2000, 33 football games were played on Thursday (a school night) to open the Division I Season. In order to compete in many of the games, students had to travel long distances and miss several days of classes. The demands of college study and rigorous practice and game schedules allow young athletes little room for social interaction or moments of socialisation with non-athletic peers. Academic studies move from centre stage in the student's life to a peripheral position somewhat akin to the place extracurricular activities normally hold.

Attempting to determine the reasons for the natural lure of athletics for young African American students and their failure to thrive in academic settings requires an understanding of:

1) the significance of a college education in America;
2) social and political links to education;
3) cultural attitudes toward African American intelligence and the black youth obsession with sports;
4) unintended social consequences; and
5) college financing and the African American Athlete.

The significance of a college degree in America

America's acknowledgment of the importance of education, seen as second only to religion from its inception as a nation-state, has been established and re-established throughout history. Among America's first European settlers in Puritan communities, the school was built immediately after the church. Education was seen as a vehicle through which to train clergy and/or community leaders. In so doing, the university assumed the role of preparing students for entry into prominent social, economic, and political positions (Rudolph, 1990). The place that education holds in the American cultural hierarchy has and continues to be a place of honour. Conversely, the established place for people of color (especially African Americans) in American Society has been and continues to be in a low social caste (Anderson, 1988; Rudolph, 1990; Bell, 1992; Hacker, 1995).

For Americans of all races and ethnic groups, a college education still affects the economic and social castes to which individuals are assigned. For African Americans and other people of color, education has also been a means of survival. The caste to which African Americans are assigned has an undeniable link to American slavery (Bell, 1992). While in slavery, African Americans were denied access to education as a means of political and social control. Anyone caught teaching a slave to read or write risked death (Anderson, 1988). When slaves were freed, education was one of the most significant privileges that African Americans sought. Leading in the early push for public education in the South, former slaves provided land and money for schools. Freedman's Bureau Superintendent John Alvord in 1866 wrote about the enthusiasm of the newly freed slaves:

'They have within themselves...a vitality and hope, coupled with patience and willingness to struggle, which foreshadows with certainty their higher education as a people in the coming time.' (Anderson, 1988, p. 15)

134 years later that hope, vitality, and willingness are still very much alive. That hope in education is regularly manifested with African American applications to institutions of higher learning. Additionally, hope, vitality, and willingness are evidenced in prominent African American professionals who have broken racial barriers in economic, social, and political venues.

Successful professionals understand the value of a long-term investment in education. Even superior athletes have an average career that lasts approximately six to ten years. For the majority of student athletes who do not make it to the rank of professional, the experience of college athletics improves them in several ways. One primary goal of higher education today, as in the past, is not knowledge but social mobility (Labaree, 1997). College athletes that earn a degree gain a distinct advantage in the job market because of this credential. According to the *Journal of Blacks in Higher Education (1999)* 'on average only 3.4 % of the civilian labour force was unemployed in 1998 (p.77)', but, as has been the case the African American unemployment rate has remained at twice the rate for whites. This has remained constant in both good and bad economic times.

Over the past 20 years, African Americans who earned a college degree greatly enhanced their prospects for employment. In 1979, only 4.3 percent of African Americans with a college degree were unemployed. African American males with only a high school diploma, during that same period had an unemployment rate of 13.6 percent. When compared with white males, the unemployment rate remained two to one with blacks and whites respectively. In 1998, the Department of Labor showed a break in the historical trend. While unemployment rates for African Americans remained constant at 2.2 times those of whites; African American unemployment for college graduates in 1998 was at 2.9 percent, only 1.7 times that of white peers. There are so few unemployed whites looking for work that the demand for any person with a college degree is strong. Historically in America, when recession hits, the rate of unemployment for African Americans, at all educational levels – rises faster and recovers at a much slower rate than that of white peers. Given these data, uneducated African Americans can hardly compete in a culture that values higher education. Gaining access and completing degree programmes is essential to African Americans who desire the benefits of entry into economic, social and potential life in the zone described as 'Middle or Upper Class'.

Cultural attitudes toward African American intelligence and the Black youth obsession with sports

When examining reasons for young college athletes to seek fame and fortune through the vehicle of professional sports, a view of one American paradox is essential. This paradox, as it portends to physical and intellectual prowess, provides a basis for understanding the need to leave the traditional educational system for a chance at American greatness. The paradox is a system that proclaims equal access based on merit; while denying equal access through discriminatory standards.

Establishing a link between political control and American meritocracy is germane to the discussion of the pervasive nature of the inculcated inferiority in poor African Americans and other children of color. Meritocracy is described as a method of earning one's place in a societal structure, due to exceptional skill or special knowledge. This concept is laudable, however Carol D. Lee (1994) indicates that:

'In the United States, political power has resided with white Anglo Saxon Protestant males since its formation as a nation state...maintaining this political dominance involves certain contradictions. It means conveying messages to the citizenry that disguise the assertion of hegemony so that it is perceived as a process of natural ordering whereby unearned privileges from racialised power relations somehow become the rewards of individual merit.' (p. 179)

If one accepts Lee's argument, grasping the rationale for the aforementioned paradox is simple. Maintaining the dominant group's control involves a system that creates and sustains winners in the dominant group. Athletics evolved as its own special world, but very much within the context of American thought. The nature of perceptions based on bigotry and bias are made exceptionally clear when examining athletics. It would appear that Blacks from the beginning would be ideal candidates for athletics. Athletes (referring to those in popular sports like football and basketball) in the early 1900s were big, strong, tough, and intellectually deficient. Dominant discourses have tended to characterise African Americans in similar ways.

When applied to education, the aforementioned system of merit also determines that any learning style that is not eurocentric in nature is flawed. Standing Bear (1938), a Native American researcher, observed the lack of vision of those in authority, when bigotry determined the agenda. He wrote :

'So we went to school to copy, to imitate; not to exchange language and ideas, and not to develop the best traits that had come out of uncountable experiences of hundreds of years of living upon this continent. Our annals, all happenings of human import, were stored in our song and dance rituals, our history differing in that it was not stored in books, but in living memory. So while the white people had much to teach us, we had much to teach them, and what a school could have been established upon that idea!' (Olquin & Schmitz, 1997: p. 437)

Just as Native American children were taught, as Standing Bear's illustrative comments indicate, that any learning that did not adhere to eurocentric standards was considered flawed, so were/are African American children taught that rhythm, movement, oral histories, and emotion have no place in academic preparation. Inculcating these notions in young disenfranchised children with different learning styles produces a sense of inferiority. This inferiority leads to a false consciousness, or the acceptance of a system that degrades and oppresses. Acceptance prompts children of color to envision themselves and their talents in the same ways that individuals like them are portrayed in the media. In fact 'media-inspired' elevation of professional athletes to the status of role models/heroes/celebrities, and the black community's association of this with 'making it' has had a noticeable effect (Gardner, 1993; Armstrong, 1994; Stanfield, 1994; Ladson-Billings, 1999; St. John, 1999).

Famed American sports writer Michael Wilbon (1997) notes the significance of a recent study:

'One...study revealed that 66 percent of all black males (in America) between the ages of 13 and 18 believe they can earn a living playing professional sports. That's more than double the proportion of white males who hold similar beliefs' (p. H1).

If this were not enough, Edwards (1999), further indicates that the push toward sports is the result of :

1) ...racist and ill-formed presumptions of race-linked athletic superiority and intellectual deficiency;
2) media propaganda portraying sports as a broadly accessible route to black social and economic mobility; and
3) a lack of comparable visible role models beyond the sports arena.

The portrayal of sports as the single positive means for African American children to gain access to America's riches is purposeful. When coupled with a sense of inferior intellectual ability, it produces a fear of academic failure and desperate attempts at any opportunity for success through merit.

In effect, the view of sports as the sole alternative to earning one's way out of poverty substantiates the notion of inferiority for children of color, reinforcing the ideals of low intellect and animal strength. To further prove that innate intellectual inferiority exists, standardized tests are utilized which, upon the surface, give the appearance of objectivity. These tests help sustain the notion of eurocentric superiority. Christopher Jencks (1998) notes five biases that coincide with eurocentric learning styles and test designers in these standardized tests. They are categorised as labelling, content, methodological, prediction and selection bias. He writes, '*Labeling bias* arises when tests claim to measure one thing but actually measure something else' (p. 55). Until 1995 the SAT stood for Scholastic Aptitude Test (Lemann, 1999). Aptitude is believed to be innate. Environment is a major factor in aptitude, which means that such tests place students from environments different from the test designer at a disadvantage (Jencks, 1998). According to Jencks:

Content bias is similar to labeling bias, but the content fails to adequately measure what the label claims to measure. *Methodological bias* arises when a test assesses mastery of some skill or body of information using a technique or method that underestimates the competence of one group relative to another. *Prediction bias* can arise whenever a test is used to predict an individual's future performance... *selection system bias* arises when three conditions are met: (1) performance depends partly on cognitive skills and partly on other traits; (2) it is easy to measure cognitive skills but hard to measure the other traits that determine performance; (3) the racial disparity in cognitive skills is larger than the racial disparity in the other, unmeasured traits that influence performance. When these three conditions hold, both educational institutions and employers have strong incentives to adopt a selection system that emphasises test scores. (Jencks, 1998, p.57)

One could reliably assume that the system is designed to maintain the status quo, and that the 'rules of engagement' will always determine who wins and who loses.

Social consequences

The previously mentioned false consciousness has had some disastrous unintended consequences. Stories abound of scandalous behaviour in collegiate sports: from drug abuse by athletes to gang rape, assaults, and theft. However, no story supports the contention that young African American athletes who leave college too soon have failed to benefit from the socialisation and emotional maturity it provides, as much as the story of Leon Smith. The Leon Smith story could have provided source material for an American success story, however this tragic narrative is one example of what can happen when students give up intellectual and social pursuits for instant riches in sports.

Leon Smith grew up in the foster care system in America. He was accepted into a major university and targeted for success. Quickly drafted into professional basketball, Smith became disgruntled the first day of practice and left the basketball court in a rage. The coach had criticised him. Smith was found later, after having swallowed 250 aspirin in a suicide attempt. He had had a nervous breakdown (Weir, 1999). Other stories may not be as tragic as Smith's, but criminal behaviour, abject poverty, chemical dependence and different types of aberrant behaviour, have resulted when athletes fail to bridge the educational, social, and emotional gaps between college athletics and professional sports (St. John, 1999).

College financing and the African American athlete

The question of whether African American athletes are given a gift when scholarships are awarded to prestigious universities or simply used as cheap labor is an important one. Almost 20 to 22 percent of public and private university funding comes from athletics (U.S. Department of Education Report, FY 1996). Faced with the possible loss of one-fifth of funding sources, colleges and universities are in strained positions when negotiating with coaches and student athletes. For a monetary outlay of about $7000.00 per year, a student athlete receives an education valued at approximately $20,000. If the athlete plays football at a Division I School, the chances are a winning season can result in a place in a Bowl Game. College Football teams playing in the Fiesta Bowl Game in 1995, received $12,000,000 each for their respective universities. 70% of the players were African Americans (Cobb, 1995).

African Americans make up over 20% of all students receiving athletic scholarships in Division I schools. Conversely, African Americans represent only six percent of the student population in the same schools (Seigal, 1996). This type of disparity is especially poignant when one realizes that this three to one ratio of African American athletes to African American students exists in the midst of the academic standards discourse. The discourse, which denies the intellectual ability of African Americans, insists that objective academic standards are never compromised, while simultaneously ignoring the standards and prevailing stereotypes to enlist African American athletes. The explanation would appear to be purely economic.

St. John (1999:1) noted that 'Except for the summer, college sports today appear on television just about every day'. The more college and university athletics are televised, the greater the revenues for institutions of higher education who take part in NCAA sports. CBS, one major American television station, paid the NCAA $1.7 billion for the rights to televise the men's Division I Basketball Championship Tournament over an eight year period. The money will be divided between NCAA member schools seen on television. Regulations established by the NCAA prohibit student athletes from receiving these funds. Many member schools, regularly seen on television with teams that are predominantly African American, have very low graduation rates for the same group. In summary, the schools get the money, and the students who regularly earn it, fail to receive either a degree or a professional contract.

Conclusions

Certain athletes enjoy popularity and become instant millionaires. The unbridled passion with which Americans admire their athletic heroes gives them celebrity status, but only in the short term. Seasoned athletes like Michael Jordan (professional basketball), Emmitt Smith (professional football), and Bo Jackson (professional baseball and football), understand the significance of a college degree, and returned to complete their higher education programmes. Acknowledging the true nature of the fleeting popularity of sports acumen and the wealth it brings, the latter successful professionals determined that higher education for African Americans has added value in the competitive American marketplace (McCallum, 1996).

NCAA Division I schools often serve as 'gatekeepers' into the professions, and ultimately the American middle and upper-class. As noted previously, even successful athletes are required to pass through the collegiate portals. When the role of gatekeeper is manipulated it helps to maintain the status quo, effectively limiting access. Additionally, continued racial animus in America, and the arbitrary standards that result, mask limited access to higher education for

African Americans and other students of color. The inconsistent manner in which these standards are applied promotes distrust and fosters challenges (Taylor, 1998; Takaki, 1997).

In the foreseeable future, given the prominence of sports, nothing exists on the horizon that will dampen the spirits of up and coming would-be athletes. Poor children of color will most likely continue to view sports as a pivotal vehicle for social status and economic mobility. As political philosophies shift from the more liberal to the conservative, access to higher education for African Americans and other students of color is even more elusive. The notion of achievement based upon merit leaves children of color in competitive situations that demand the use of any skills that can gain them advantage.

The continued financial woes of colleges and universities give credence to the argument that there will be a need for revenue producing activities. Athletic competition has satisfactorily bridged the gap for institutions of higher learning for a time. African American athletes and others who receive a college education succeed in passing through the portal toward a better life. When both athletes and colleges benefit, the system works at its best, however one problem still remains. The absence of substantive dialogue on the issue of race in America serves to affect every facet of American life. Higher education is no exception. The need for scholars to take the lead in such discussions is more pronounced than ever before. Unfortunately, racial dialogue in academe too often gives way to stereotypical perceptions and racial myths, and America's intellectuals also slip into the abyss of racism, failing to educate many athletes of color.

References

Anderson, J. D. (1988) *The education of Blacks in the South, 1860-1935*, Chapel Hill, The University of North Carolina Press.

Armstrong, T. A. (1994) *Multiple intelligences in the classroom*, Alexandria, VA, Association for Supervision and Curriculum Development.

Bell, D. (1992) *Faces at the bottom of the well: the permanence of racism*, New York, BasicBooks.

Cobb, G. (1995, October) 'Unpaid Black athletes remain slaves on campuses' *The Philadelphia Tribune*, 86,6-A.

Dempsey, C.W. (1999) 'A letter from Cedric W. Dempsey, NCAA President' in http:// www.ncaa.org/eligibility/cbsa/

Edwards, H. (1994a, December) 'The BCA-NCAA Rift: A meaningful resolution is unlikely' in *Sport*, 70.

Edwards, H. (1994b, July) 'Black youths' commitment to sports achievement: a virtue-turned-tragic-turned-virtue' in *Sport*, 86.

Edwards, H. (1999, May) 'An end of the golden age of Black participation in sports' in Tennessee *Tribune* 9, 2A.

Gardner, H. (1993) *Multiple intelligences: the theory in practice*, New York, BasicBooks.

Hacker, A. (1992) *Two nations: black and white separate, hostile, unequal*, New York, Ballentine Books.

Jencks, C. (1998) 'Racial bias in testing' in Jencks, C. & Phillips, M. (eds). *The Black-White test score gap*, Washington, D.C., Brookings, 55-85.

Labaree, David. (1997, Spring). 'Public goods, private goods: the American struggle'. Over educational goals in *American Educational Research Journal*, 34 (1): 39-81.

Ladson-Billings, G. (2000) 'Racialized discourses and ethnic epistemologies' in Denzin, K. and Lincoln, Y. (eds) *Handbook of Qualitative Research Second Edition*, Thousand Oaks, Sage, 257-278.

Lemann, Nicholas. (1999, September 6) 'Behind the SAT' in *Newsweek,* 52.

Lee, C. D. (1994) 'African-centered pedagogy: complexities and possibilities' in Shujaa, M. (ed) *Too much schooling, too little education: a paradox of Black life in White societies*, Trenton, Africa World Press, 295-318.

McCallum, J. (1996) 'Better late than never. (Athletes and College Degrees)' in *Sports Illustrated*, 84, 72.

NCAA Graduation Rates Summary (1998) http://www.ncaa.org/grad_rates/

Olquin, E. and Schmitz, B. (1997) 'Transforming the curriculum through diversity' in Gaff, J. and Radcliff, L. and Associates (eds) *Handbook of the undergraduate curriculum: A comprehensive guide to purpose, structures, practices, and change*, San Francisco, Jossey-Bass Publishers.

Rudolph, F. (1990) *The American college & university: a history*, Athens, The University of Georgia Press.

Siegel, D. (1996) 'Higher education and the plight of the Black male athlete' in Lapchick, R.E. (ed) *Sport in society: equal opportunity or business as usual?* Thousand Oaks, Sage, 17-34.

Stanfield, J. H. (1994) 'Ethnic modeling in qualitative research' in Denzin, N. & Lincoln, Y. (eds) *Handbook of qualitative research*, Thousand Oaks, Sage Publications, Inc., 175-188

St. John, E. (1999, April) 'Collegiate athletic highlights' in B*lack issues in higher education*, 80-86.

Takaki, Ronald (1997) 'Asian Americans: the myth of the model minority' in Skolnick, J. and Currie, E. (eds) *Crisis in American institutions*, New York, Longman, 174-180.

U. S. Department of Education (1995-96) 'Finance, FY96' Survey in *Integrated Postsecondary Education Data System (IPEDS)*, National Center for Education Statistics.

'Vital signs: are the athletic powerhouses ignoring the education of Black athletes?' (1999) in The Journal Of Blacks in Higher Education , 22, 77 http://www.softlineweb.com/ softlineweb/b

Weir, Tom (1999, November 26) 'Direct leap to the NBA too high For Smith despite physical gifts, troubled teen not ready, Mavericks' Nelson says *USA Today,* 1C.

Wilbon, Michael (1997, March 22) 'Dreams of pros are a con " *Washington Post,* H1, H4.

137

Chapter Eleven

Evaluating the role of life skills in successful participation

Robin Gutteridge

Introduction

This chapter presents some tentative conclusions drawn from a number of years of work in widening participation and enhancing student retention. Continuous advances in knowledge, a political and economic climate of limited funding and a growing culture of accountability with, laudably, an emphasis on anti-discriminatory practice mean that maintaining quality of the learning experience in higher education is an increasingly complex issue. Rivis (1996) argues that changes in Government policy, patterns of entry to HE and in the organisation and delivery of education have focused attention to quality and effectiveness of the learning experience and also generated increased demands for student support, advice and guidance.

One aspect of quality is the tensions arising from the support needs of students who manage additional needs or difference. Students may be managing a health difficulty, a disability, the effects of a disadvantaged or atypical entry profile, or the cumulative impact of a combination of such factors. Meeting their needs may create tensions for the institution because equality of opportunity and educational pedagogy demands integration and yet such students may be costly to support. They may also expose deficiencies, prejudice and weaknesses in the structures and values, which support the educational system (Heron 1997).

'With great financial pressure on institutions to maximise fee income and to educate students at lowest cost, there is a strong disincentive for institutions to accept any student requiring costly additional support.' (Educare June 1990, p13).

Equal opportunities and equity demand recognition of the cumulative disadvantage which may limit access and entitlement for these students. For instance, existing literature suggests that adults with disabilities who choose to study may be disadvantaged educationally, financially and socially by a long social history of segregation and exclusion (French, 1993, Scullion, 1995). This tends to generate a cycle which becomes a self-fulfilling prophecy of non-participation and may mean that entering higher education is fraught with difficulties related to negative prior experiences, low self image and limited knowledge on which to base expectations of study.

Social welfare research suggests a strong correlation between membership of a minority group and exclusion or limited participation in the rights and responsibilities of citizenship. Since universities are social organisations which reflect the values and structures of the wider society in which they exist, (Kolb, 1984; Morgan, 1997; Helman 1997) it is not surprising that this trend is repeated in Higher Education, where members of all the recognised minority groups are under-represented. (Stapleford and Todd 1997, Swain *et al* 1993, French 1993, Finkelstein 1990, Oliver 1993, Bheenuck et al 1998, Darr 1998, Gutteridge and Crompton 1998, The Chartered Society of Physiotherapy 2000, Harrison 2000, Richhariya-Leahy 2000, Sharples and McAndrew 2000). Much work to enhance recruitment and retention among marginalised groups focuses around enhancing the recruitment and on-course support of students with disabilities, students of black and Asian ethnic origin and students from low socio-economic groups or disadvantaged educational backgrounds.

However, the increasing costs of offering high quality and appropriate support may not be restricted to students with additional needs. Changing social norms, parental concerns about safety and the enhanced expectations of a consumer society may result in decreased entry skills. According to Marchbank and Letherby (2000), students who arrive with limited life skills or coping strategies tend to make greater demands on academic and support staff for pastoral and practical care. A study by Monk and Robson (1999) suggests that life skills development is necessary in students:

'The areas where training was most needed were, unsurprisingly, financial management, communication, language, discipline, reliability, motivation, social skills, personal hygiene and the less 'headline worthy' health issues such as hepatitis.' (Monk and Robson 1999 p335)

Existing literature tends both to consider members of minority groups as if their needs were homogeneous and to neglect the possibility of common factors between groups. Although apparently a contradictory statement, this chapter draws together the findings and recommendations from a variety of sources relating to higher education to propose that strategies for promotion of more equitable participation are likely to demonstrate greater effectiveness if knowledge, learning and experience between groups is shared more widely. They are especially likely to be successful when they take account of the skills development and coping strategies of the individual and the demands made upon these coping skills at different stages of access and participation. It is not suggested that such measures will eliminate the significant and cumulative barriers to participation imposed by structural disadvantage such as poverty or discrimination. Rather, it is proposed that initiatives to deconstruct structural barriers are more likely to be successful if the individual perspective is considered alongside wider social factors.

This chapter argues that lack of life skills may be a significant factor in supporting under-representation and their development is a key factor in redressing the balance. It is suggested that life skills of self-appraisal, communication and self-management are crucial for all students for effective coping with the experience of higher education. Further, it is argued that though relevant for all students, such skills are especially important to students who have any characteristic which singles them out from the norm.

For each student, motivation and approach to study, as well as academic progress will depend on their personal context. The learner must be viewed as a unique individual with different support needs, but also with needs which vary at different stages in their engagement. Nevertheless, there are common characteristics among student cohorts, which enable consideration of particular and key aspects of study support (Gutteridge and Crompton 1998). Tait (1994) argues that 'An educational methodology which does not recognise the situation of its learners denies and diminishes them.' However, Marchbank and Letherby (2000) question the extent to which it is reasonable or possible to expect even the most supportive Higher Education institution to take responsibility for addressing inadequacies in life skills among their learners.

Evidence base

The discussion presented in this chapter is not derived from a single traditional research report. Instead, findings and recommendations are extracted from a number of studies. These are combined with expert opinion derived from planning, review, quality and staff development sources. The author has been associated with each of the studies used, either as a primary researcher, a collaborative researcher or as a contributor. Because the author had been involved in each study and had been instrumental in determining or directing the philosophy, aims and focus of each source of evidence used, it is possible to be certain that comparable definitions and underpinning assumptions influenced each study. To that extent at least, the studies cited are consistent, thus addressing one of the key weaknesses often found in the use of multiple sources.

All studies used a qualitative method and focus on evaluation of the effectiveness of advice and guidance work in undergraduate admissions or student support. Qualitative enquiry values subjectivity and integrates reflexivity within the interpretative framework (Strauss and Corbin 1988). A reflexive process continuously challenges assumptions made by the researcher in order to examine whether they may reflect inappropriate socially constructed beliefs and attitudes. Qualitative methods were particularly helpful in generating the discussion presented in this chapter because of this continuous challenge but also because they are effective in investigating the individual and personal perspective, especially where little is known. Additionally, they do not seek to generalise findings to a whole population and so tend to generate understanding of the lived experience, promoting further discussion, together with tentative theory and hypothesis development, all of which may be open to further and wider testing by different methods. They are thus ideal for investigating little known or understood phenomena (Banister *et al.* 1994, Oiler Boyd 1990, Polit and Hungler 1995). This chapter concentrates not on the well identified structural barriers which may restrict participation and undermine retention, but on the little understood personal and individual factors which may undermine the success of initiatives to redress the structural imbalances. In particular, this chapter seeks to draw together findings from work exploring different dimensions of structural disadvantage. It does so in order to evaluate the opportunities for learning and enhanced understanding of the complex personal and social interactions which may limit participation and to use this understanding for the benefit of all students.

Two locations were used for the studies cited; a traditional, medium sized city-centre university campus and also the Open University, which uses a model of supported Open Learning with students undertaking the majority of study in their own home, albeit with regular access to tutorial and tutor support. Much of the evidence is derived from work with students with disabilities or learning skills needs. A relatively small amount of work is specifically with students from ethnic minority groups, but the studies conducted with whole cohorts of students do contain members of minority groups which reflect the demographic distribution in the UK. However, a considerable proportion of the students who contributed to the findings in this chapter were managing the cumulative effects of multiple disadvantage or social exclusion. For example, many students had experienced the effects of multi-generation poverty, of discrimination or inequality of opportunity as well as managing the impact of a disability or non- standard educational background.

Table 1 summarises the research work from which this chapter is derived.

Table 1. Studies which comprise the evidence base for the discussion

Date & location of study	Focus of study	Sample Number	Sample Characteristic	Method
1997 Open Learning Environment (Gutteridge and Crompton 1998)	Student support Staff Development Collaborative method	10 students 10 subject tutors	Student with significant motor or sensory impairment and their module tutor	Qualitative Reflective diary plus Reflective interview at key points plus Focus Group
1994 -1998 Open Learning Environment	Study support needs	120 students	Student with health difficulty or disability	Qualitative interview plus survey
1999-2000 Campus University	Post Admission/ Induction evaluation	192 students	Standard and non-standard entrants two student cohorts, representative of demographic pattern	Mixed method survey followed by selective qualitative interview
1999-2000 Campus University	Study support needs assessment/ Evaluation	5 unsuccessful applicants and 15 students	Applicant or student with health difficulty or disability	Qualitative interviews
1997-2000 mixed locations	Staff development	25 academic and academic support staff	Expert workers with learning and disability support	Qualitative interviews plus focus groups
1996-1998 Open Learning environment	Learning support	60 students	Students with learning skills development needs	Qualitative interviews, reflective diaries
1998-2000 Campus University	Learning support	12 students	Students with learning skills development needs	Qualitative interviews, reflective Diaries
2000 Campus University (Harrison 2000)	Student poverty: a factor in retention	30 students	Year One and Year Three Health Sciences students	Focus Groups
1995- 2000 mixed locations	Needs of ethnic minority group members	9 students	Students self referred with a study difficulty attributed to ethnic background	Qualitative interview
1994-2000 mixed locations	Needs of gay, lesbian or bisexual students	6 students	Students self referred with a study difficulty attributed to their sexuality	Qualitative interview

Results

The findings were very similar among students with different characteristics. This applied whether they were identified as having additional needs or had experienced a more normative social development. Even students who perceived themselves to be confident in their coping skills or who reported high personal self identity or self esteem showed similar results

The vast majority of students were satisfied or very satisfied with their choice of institution and the quality of advice, guidance and support services. Despite this, every single student interviewed reported some difficulty preparing appropriately for entry, accessing meaningful advice and guidance before and during study and in managing study alongside their daily life. Each student described anxiety and fears accompanying the recognition that their personal skills were sometimes inadequate for the task they had set themselves. Every student described the difficulties inherent in this personal insight and a subsequent set of difficulties related to seeking help, advice and support. Students with additional needs, or who perceived themselves to be different to the norm were especially likely to report difficulties, or to report multiple difficulties or anxieties which cumulatively affected their study or their integration into university life.

The results of these studies suggest three main dimensions of life skills most crucial to successful participation.

Successful participation. Three key dimensions of life skills

There appeared to be three main aspects of life skills which may be important predictors of successful participation. These were the ability to manage self, in terms of time management and organisation, the ability to appraise one's own situation and evaluate progress or needs and finally, the communication skills necessary to interact with the world and especially, with the organisation. Each of these will be described in more detail, but it must be emphasised that to a greater or lesser extent, all the key dimensions interact with one another, resulting in yet a further layer of disadvantage for students who lack skills in any dimension, or flexibility in integrating these skills.

Self management

The skill of effectively managing self included all the dimensions of organising and managing a domestic and social life as well as the demands of a study programme. These included skills such as time management and juggling conflicting priorities to enable efficient and stress free progress through the day, the week and the study year. Co-ordinating support mechanisms was an additional layer of management which placed extra demands on students with identified additional needs, perhaps because of a disability. Managing, for example, the task of establishing new social networks at the same time as developing a routine with a helper is a very complex skill in self management

Self- appraisal

Self-appraisal incorporated the ability honestly to evaluate one's own performance and progress and to act upon personal reflection and external advice to make changes or adjustments in a number of behavioural and skills domains. These included constant evaluation of 'fit' between the expectations and demands of the course and individual skills base, the ability and willingness to recognise the need for help and the confidence to act upon that recognition. Such self-appraisal demands considerable maturity and insight which cannot always be assumed and which takes many people a lifetime to develop. To employ appropriate help seeking behaviour demands a great deal in terms of confidence and interpersonal skills, not to mention skills of analysis, review and planning together with considerable study skills. Finally, the ability to implement agreed or perceived necessary change and continuously to review progress demands considerable motivation and tenacity.

Communication skills

The third life skill identified as a key predictor of successful participation was the ability to communicate effectively with peers, tutors in order to manage organisational structures, daily life and the teaching and learning experience. Communication skills perceived to be important included the ability to articulate the problem and to negotiate a solution. Assertiveness skills appeared to be very important, together with skills of appropriate self-disclosure and overall, competence in interpersonal skills.

Students expected the institution to provide easy access to meaningful information about advice, guidance and support, together with rapid response to a disclosure of need. Disturbingly, even with insight or direct advice, students still tend not to access channels of support such as study skills development material. They prefer to seek one to one advice and support, with the result that popular or 'helpful' staff become overloaded. There may be a number of reasons for this behaviour, but some students feel unable to take responsibility for their own decisions:

'When I've got a problem, I want someone to help me decide what to do. I don't really want to have to work it out for myself. It takes too long and I might get it wrong. I want someone to share the blame.' (Standard entry year 2 resit student)

'I was unprepared. Not the work, but coping with my life and all the added extras; it's no-one else's responsibility to manage some of these things, I see that now. I was advised to develop some of my skills before embarking on the course... I need to go away and learn how to live and then come back free to concentrate on study. I can't learn to do both at the same time, no matter how much support I get.'
(Student with a disability, withdrawing)

The perceived attitude to disclosure of need was important. Predictably, students who felt disclosure would be perceived punitively were less likely to disclose or seek help until driven by a crisis. However, a perceived negative attitude was often at variance with evidence from the written information and response of the staff. Students often reported being surprised and encouraged at the actual response to their disclosure. Fear of the effect of the disclosure appears to be inhibitory.

'I find it really hard to ask for help. I feel I'm being a nuisance. No one gives me that impression, it's how I feel.' (Year One student with a disability, during Term 3)

Students may disregard or discount advice, perceiving it not to be applicable to their situation:

'I was warned but I had no idea I would be so busy, so tired and that organising my own food, shopping and life would take so much time.'
(Standard entry 18 year old Year 1 student, six weeks into study)

'The information I was given was quite clear; I just didn't believe it.'
(Standard entry Year 1 student, post induction evaluation.)

The first six weeks after the start of the course were identified quite clearly as the most difficult period where financial and social resources are at their most limited, while anxiety and expectations for academic and social integration highest of all. Students reported strong feelings of vulnerability, exclusion, isolation and anxiety during this early part of the course.

It is difficult to manage such emotions while tired the investment of time and energy the multiple demands in an unfamiliar context require. In other words, their coping strategies and support networks were at the least effective exactly at the time of highest demand.

The most difficult thing is not the work, it's getting myself organised.'
(Year 1 student, with a disability, 6 weeks after entry)

'It was okay at school, everything was organised for me, but here I have to manage my time, arrange to eat, do laundry, negotiate a relationship with my helper and manage the invoices for my helper support and equipment. There's loads of help but I'm not used to taking responsibility for co-ordinating everything.'
(Year 1 student with a disability, end of year interview)

'It all seemed to hit me at once; arranging my room, finding my way round, making new friends, fitting in, managing the work, even finding a lecturer's office so you could ask for help… just knocking on a door to look for an unfamiliar face.… and on top of all that, doing my washing, finding the supermarket, cooking after a full day in class.. I never realised how much my mum does.. and she works full time too. It has really increased my respect for her…'
(Standard entry Year 1 student, reflecting on term 1)

'It's all the little things like… my computing equipment arrived, no problem, but how do you unpack it and put it together from a wheelchair. I've never used a computer. And where do you store the boxes in a tiny flat? I needed a man to appear with the kit!
(Year 4 open learning student in middle years of life, wheelchair user)

Managing life and the consequent demands on skills of self-appraisal and communication appeared to pose particular concern.

'I got told off for being late for the first three tutorials on the trot. I simply didn't have [the courage] to explain it was because the car park attendant had forgotten to meet me.. even though it had been arranged in advance. It annoyed me to think I was being labelled through no fault of my own, especially when I had invested so much effort in getting there in the first place…'

(50 year old female student with a disability, new to study)
'I can't think about anything else; I know I need to study more than most and I'm getting behind but sorting out this thing is a life issue and it seems more important at the moment.'
(18 year old non standard entry student struggling with identity crisis)

'I'm so homesick I can't function.'
(Year 1 student from rural area, 11 weeks into the course, on moving to a medium sized city)

Earlier experience was recognised as a source of disadvantage

'It's hard to know what is a difficulty because I'm from a different culture and English is my second language and what is a difficulty because I don't grasp the subject.'
(Year 2 resit student of Asian origin)

'Everyone else knew how to behave in a pub but I've never been in one and my parents would haul me home if they knew I'd visited one; I kept looking over my shoulder the whole evening; I couldn't enjoy it but I so want to fit in. I couldn't tell anyone how I felt.'
(Year 1 student, from a strict religious community)

' My father was in the Armed Forces. We moved from school to school. It helps me to settle down in a new environment more quickly but it also means I never grasped the basic rules of grammar.'
(Year 1 mature student, spelling and reading age equivalent to 13 years, no evidence of specific learning difficulty)

'I coped by working longer and harder but there comes a point where there aren't any more hours in the day.'
(Year 2 student, diagnosed as dyslexic after crisis)

The cumulative impact of anxieties was keenly recognised:

'The money isn't the biggest thing: it's just the final straw on top of everything else.'
(Year 1 student in financial difficulty and family difficulties, later supported without withdrawing.)

'It's fine as long as no-one in the family is sick and my support networks all work. And everything falls apart at exam time... always!'
(Mature female student with caring role, Year 2)

Some students however, appeared comfortable with their lack of skills:

'I've never used a washing machine, public transport, or cooked anything other than beans on toast. I don't intend to start learning now; I'm too busy. I've been posting my washing home. My dad will come and get me when I want to visit home and I eat in the canteen.'
(Standard entry year 1 student)

I'm here to study, not organise my life. My social worker does the rest.'
(18 year old student with physical impairment)

Discussion

It could be argued that a strong academic baseline will mediate for a paucity of life skills, but this is likely to be a fallacious assumption. This point is supported by a key difference in the characteristics of students between the two institutions featured. One has an open entry policy, with no academic entry requirements. A significant proportion of the student body comprise people who have little or no experience of formal education beyond the statutory minimum, though they may have gained considerable skills and experience through their life and employment experience. In contrast, the other university has more traditional entry requirements. The particular course undertaken by all the students featured has among the highest and most stringent entry requirements in the university and is very competitive nationally. Around one third of this student group are also mature entrants with non-standard academic backgrounds and significant life skills, who have nevertheless also developed a strong academic baseline. Despite these differences in academic attainment, the findings between the different groups of students were remarkably similar, though, perhaps significantly, students without experience of the world of work were overwhelmingly more likely to report perceived inadequacies in their life skills.

Rather than considering membership of a minority group as the key predictor of need and under-representation, it is argued that group membership is a factor which may increase the risk of a particular type of need or disadvantage being encountered. If present, such a need or disadvantage is likely to contribute to under –representation, either at access or in terms of retention. Membership of a minority group does not itself automatically ensure the experience of disadvantage. Instead, it is suggested that students who may be at risk from disadvantage include all those who have life experiences or support needs significantly different from the average or norm, or where there is a discrepancy between the expectations of the institution and the entry profile of the student.

This possibility applies to all students, and so it is proposed that the individual and their life course become a very important aspect of needs assessment in developing a learning plan for any student. The likelihood of cumulative disadvantage appears to be greater from members of minority groups because their life experiences may not have permitted equal access to opportunities for the development of core life skills expected to be present on entry. Thus it is proposed that the barriers to participation in higher education arise not only a direct result of the structural barriers encountered by members of minority groups in the wider population, which may result in a cumulative disadvantage. Barriers may also result from the way all individuals react to and learn from their life experiences. Many strategies to widen participation or to enhance retention do not consider the interaction of both aspects of disadvantage in their joint effect on student participation, progress and retention.

If individuals do not acquire the skills necessary to manage higher education before arrival, for whatever reason this may occur, simplistic strategies to enhance retention, such as increasing funding may not be as effective as they might otherwise be. Similarly, strategies to widen participation which redress poverty, or unfamiliarity with the context may be more successful if they also take account of the extent to which an individual student still needs help to develop communication skills, or time management skills. If these skills are significantly lacking on arrival, it is possible that continuing initiatives to widen participation, together with increasing recruitment competition between institutions may simply generate the type of increasing demands on pastoral and academic staff described by Marchbank and Letherby (2000). The transition into higher education is demanding even for the best prepared and advantaged student. It is unreasonable to expect students to develop significant life skills at the same time as managing that transition. There are many excellent models of education which do consider personal and life skills development alongside academic development. It is suggested that co-operation and collaboration between sectors may enable a more holistic needs based consideration of student support. Such a model could take account not only of structural barriers but also of personal coping mechanisms and strategies which could be built upon, as well as prompting a broad based individual development action plan or learning agreement. This would be easily transferable between institutions or sectors, and might be as integral to selection procedures as the academic benchmarks currently used. Furthermore, true equality of opportunity prompts greater acknowledgement of the possibility that all students may benefit from such individual skills development programmes.

Towards a new definition of additional deeds

Additional needs is a term often used to describe students whose needs for extra support arise from a disability or health difficulty. It is suggested that the term could be used more globally to describe the needs of any student whose skills, academic baseline or experience varies from the normative expectation of the institution. Such redefinition may assist clearer analysis and understanding of the diversity of additional support needs and may support a classification of student by need rather than by minority group membership. This is important because analysis and understanding of the nature of the additional need is crucial to the design of an appropriate action plan to redress under-representation. It is a stereotypical assumption, for instance, that all students with disabilities will require study support, or that standard entrants will not have needs for additional study skills development.

According to the broader definition proposed, students with additional needs may be argued as those whose health status, way of functioning in activities of daily living, skills base, social or cultural background or support structures makes participation in Higher Education more difficult, unusual or time consuming than the average student. The average student does not exist, but all institutions design their programmes with an image of the average or normative student in mind. Using this broader definition, students with additional needs would include those who have learning or life skills which do not fully equip them for the demands or expectations of their course. It would also include those who have a disability or health difficulty, those for whom Higher Education is an alien culture or environment, and those whose social origin or status makes them a minority in terms of proportional representation in the student population. It could also incorporate those students whose social support structures, whether personal or financial, are not sufficient for their needs.

Yeo (1996) suggests that two conflicting paradigms currently exist within higher education. The humanist paradigm views the student as a beneficiary, rather than a participant and gives rise to a paternalistic model of provision, while the systems paradigm is grounded in a culture of accountability and tends to lead to an administrative model of service provision. Neither paradigm may accurately reflect the actual needs of learners, especially those with a history of non-participation or exclusion from the rights and responsibilities of citizenship. Instead, a life course collaborative model which links the learner and their learning experiences throughout life into a planned and cumulative progression of skills development may be a more appropriate way of ensuring successful participation.

Conclusion

This chapter does not argue that structural barriers to participation can be addressed by a focus on life skills development. To do so would be a facile and destructive affirmation of the social constructions which support exclusion and disadvantage. It is argued that strategies to enhance student participation, support or progress within higher education are likely to be of limited success if developed without consideration of social context, both organisational and individual. From this perspective, it is suggested that consideration of the disadvantage not only of structural barriers but also of resultant or accompanying lack of life skills development. Such consideration may promote more effective strategies and initiatives to widen participation and enhance retention by considering the cumulative impact of individual previous learning experience and focusing attention also towards ensuring the individual has the opportunity and necessary support to develop their individual life skills and their coping skills.

Advice, guidance and strategies to widen participation are integral to retention. The institution actively influences the probability of retention from the moment the student first becomes aware of its existence. However, retention is affected, and may be determined long before the first enquiry by the previous life course learning the student has (or has not) experienced. The extent to which a higher education institution is able to address the need for life skills development at the same time as facilitating academic learning will perhaps depend to a great extent to the investment of resource in technology, staff development, and pastoral care provision (Gutteridge and Crompton 1998).

The message of this chapter is underlined by an extract from an UK Government policy document:

'In the move towards a learning society, with an economy driven by high level skills and knowledge based industries, higher education will have a central role. But it will only be fully effective if it succeeds in making its students into autonomous lifelong learners. This requires a judicious balance of services, on one hand to help learners develop skills of self-management, and on the other to help them make immediate decisions about learning and work. These services need to be seen as a whole, underpinning lifelong learning and central to the purposes of higher education. The learning society depends on autonomous individuals, able to manage their lifelong learning and working careers efficiently and confidently' (DfEE 1997).

References

Banister, P., Burman, E., Parker, I., Taylor, M. and Tindall, C. (1994). Qualitative methods in psychology *A Research Guide*. Open University Press, Buckingham.

Bheenuck, S., Coles, J., Means, R., Sherratt, D., Senior, B. and Upton, T. (1998). Report of a working group into facilitating access for Black and minority ethnic students into the NHS professions, *Faculty of Health and Social Care*, University of the West of England, Bristol.

Chartered Society of Physiotherapy, (2000). *Widening Participation*, Report to Working Party examining under-representation, July 2000, London.

Darr, A. (1998). *Improving the Recruitment and Retention of Asian Students on Nursing, Midwifery, Radiography and Physiotherapy Courses*, A Qualitative research Report prepared for The University of Bradford School of Healthcare Studies, December 1998, Bradford, England.

Department for Education and Employment, (1997). *Getting the most out of HE: Supporting Learner Autonomy, a briefing paper for Higher Education and Employment*, November 1997, p27.

Educare (1990). Editorial comment, *Educare*, June 1990, p13.

Finkelstein, V. (1990). *Disability-Changing Practice*, home study text X for K665, The Disabling Society, The Open University, Milton Keynes, p25-26.

French, S. (1993), *Dismantling the Barriers*, K665, The Disabling Society, Workbook 3, Open University Press, Buckingham.

Gutteridge R., and Crompton, S. (1998). Setting up a regional resource bank of skills, knowledge and information to enhance the support of disabled students. *A pilot study*, Internal research report for the Open University, Milton Keynes.

Harrison, K. (2000). *An Exploration of the Relationship Between Student Finance and Student Withdrawal at Coventry University*, A project report prepared by the Head of Physiotherapy Subject Group for the Senior Pro-Vice Chancellor, Coventry University.

Helman, C. (1997). *Culture, Health and Illness*, 3rd edn., Butterworth Heinemann, Oxford.

Heron, M. (1997). *Researching reality, meaning, change and growth in the Open University*. Abridged version of 'In my own skin' presented at the launch of the Open University Centre for Educational Guidance and Student Support, 24 Oct 1997.

Kolb, D. (ed.), (1984). *Organisational Psychology*, Prentice Hall, New York.

Marchbank, J. and Letherby, G. (2000). Offensive and defensive: feminist pedagogy, student support and higher education evaluation, in Howie G and Tauchert A., (eds)., (in press). *Feminist Pedagogy*, Ashgate, UK.

Monk, A.S. and Robson, I.B.(1999). The increase of psycho-social and stress-related problems in UK agricultural colleges; the wardens' experience, *Journal of Further and Higher Education*, Vol 23, No 3, p335.

Morgan, G. (1997). *Images of Organization*, Sage, London.

Oiler-Boyd, J. (1990). Qualitative approaches to research in LoBiondo-Wood G., Haber J., (eds.), (1992). Nursing Research: Methods, Critical Appraisal and Utilisation, 2nd edn., Mosby, St Louis.

Oliver, M. (1993). *Disability, Citizenship and Empowerment*, Workbook 2 in K665, The Disabling Society, The Open University, Milton Keynes.

Polit, D. and Hungler, B. (1997). Essentials of Nursing Research, Lippincott, Philadelphia.

Richhariya-Leahy, S. (2000). *Clinical Placement Access Evaluation for Students with (Physical and Sensory) Impairments*, HEFCE funded project in process, dissemination conference at University of Leeds School of Healthcare Studies, March 2000.

Rivis, V. (1996). Assuring the Quality of Guidance and Learner Support in Higher Education, Chapter 1 in Wisker G. and Brown S., (eds.), (1996). *Enabling Student Learning Systems and Strategies*, Kogan Page in Association with the Staff and Educational Development Association, London.

Scullion, P. (1995). Oliver asks for more; rejecting illness, neglecting impairment, explaining disability and controlling rehabilitation, Editorial in *British Journal of Therapy and Rehabilitation*, October 1995, Vol 2, No10, P521 -522.

Sharples, N. and McAndrw, P. (2000). *Deaf People's Access to Nurse Education*, Paper prepared for the ENB, March 2000.

Stapelford, J. and Todd, C., (1997). *Entry of Black Students into the Professions Allied to Medicine*, Conference Paper given at the Alliance for Health Professionals Conference December 1987, Work undertaken at Leeds Metropolitan University, Leeds, UK

Strauss, A.,. and Corbin, J. (1998). *Basics of Qualitative Research* (2nd edn.), Sage, London

Swain, J. Finkelstein V., French S., Oliver M., (1993). *Disabling Barriers, Enabling Environments*. Open University Press, Buckingham.

Tait, A. (1994). The End of innocence: critical approaches to open and distance learning. *Open Learning*, 9,3 Nov, pp 27-39.

Yeo, S. (1996). Learning materialism, *Adult Learning*, Vol 7, No5, Jan, p107-110.

Chapter Twelve

From information poor to information rich: can the electronic university reach the hard to reach?

Sue Webb

Introduction: conceptualisations of new learning technologies and adult learning

Information technology skills have become a new form of literacy for the 21st century, and increasingly practice to widen participation to higher education is utilising the Internet for the delivery of information and guidance to under-represented groups (HEFCE, 1999; Wiseman and Kendall, 2000). In other words, the policy discourse of widening participation seems to have assimilated the notion that new learning technologies facilitate access and participation. As a consequence, I will argue that flexible learning has become the 'condensation symbol' (Edelman, 1977) or shorthand descriptor for Internet and web-based learning and a central feature of strategies to widen participation and ensure lifelong learning. How has this happened? Do these strategies work?

There is no easy answer to these questions because the impact that these strategies will have on adult education and widening participation has been woefully under-explored (Boshier, 1999; Gorard and Selwyn, 1999). This chapter will suggest that frequently policy and practice has focused on the technical or quantitative aspects of access, such as ensuring that facilities are available to all, rather than on the qualitative. In contrast, a focus on the latter would consider the factors affecting who makes the choice to use these new technologies for learning, and why, and who can be effective in using them, and why. In order to assess the extent to which educational policy and practice are able to encourage the information poor to become information rich, this paper examines on the one hand, recent policy documents from the UK and on the other hand, research literature and practice in the use of communications and information technology in adult and higher education. By examining the discourses of lifelong learning and new technologies in education it considers not just 'thin' access questions about the availability of new equipment and of education and training to learn how to use it, but also 'thick' access questions about 'access for whom, access to what and for what purpose?' (Burbules and Callister, 2000:21).

New learning technologies and lifelong learning policy, practice, and research: the making of the discourses

Standard analyses of the relationship between policy making and research refer to the politicisation of this process whereby policy and decision making are developed on the basis of the infiltration and assimilation of ideas by key players, or the slow accretion of the perspectives of a number of selected research findings, experiences and other ideas, rather than as a result of a rational assessment to apply the learning from specific studies (Weiss and Bucuvalas, 1980). Drawing on this approach to policy development this paper will argue that lifelong learning and flexible learning utilising new technologies, have become connotive and central to strategies to widening participation. Such linkages have been possible because these concepts are fluid and have been invested with different meanings by different players. For example, overviews of lifelong learning and the learning society have identified shifts in meaning and emphasis from those that have focused on learning in industrial societies as a condition of and for equal opportunities, in other words, the democratic and citizenship model, to those that since the mid-1970s have linked learning to the health of economies, that is to the human capital model (Edwards, 1997) or what Jarvis has called *work*life learning (Jarvis, 2000). However, it is a shift marked by contestation (Edwards, 1997) in which some researchers identify a discursive space in which 'broader and more transformative' conceptualisations can be developed (Strain and Field, 1997:153) or as Coffield (1997:454) has summarised,

'The researchers....not only want to take the Learning Society to the cleaners but wish to change the use to which it is put from developing utopian modules of the future to a means of assessing and improving on the present'.

Somekh (2000, 20) suggests that 'politicians have taken possession of the new technology image and offered it to the electorate as a talisman' and she identifies a discontinuity between the enthusiasm of politicians and committed educational innovators, and research and evaluation into its effectiveness. However, this analysis of policy tends to assume a realist stance, and focuses on the failure of the policy and practice to match up to research 'truths'. Another way of making sense of this discontinuity is to regard the politicisation of new technologies for education not as an example of the ideological power of politicians but as an outcome of the meaning making processes that politicians, practitioners and researchers are engaged in. This discursive approach to policy analysis draws on the work of Foucault and the arguments for its application to education, and more specifically adult education and lifelong learning (Ball, 1990; Nicoll, 1999; and Usher and Edwards, 1994).

In developing such an analysis I am mindful that this paper provides an account that also seeks to construct the 'reality' about 'what is going on' when new learning technologies are linked to widening participation strategies. In my practice as a lecturer and curriculum developer in continuing education, increasingly my day to day support of students is conducted on-line, whilst whole modules are provided via the Internet and seminars are virtual. In other words, it is a practice that acknowledges that these media have challenged notions of locality and proximity. Positioned in these ways, I am an enthusiast who is ready to accept the arguments that a third generation of distance learning based on these communication technologies has developed which offers a solution to many of the structural barriers that adult learners experience of lack of time, availability, geographical distance and inflexible provision (Halal and Liebowitz, 1994; Laurillard, 1993; McConnell, 1998). However, other more sceptical discourses persist that draw on evaluations of new technologies in education which point to the need for a cultural change in institutions and for more staff development if these technologies are to make a difference to learning (Banks and McConnell, 2000; Somekh, 2000).

The starting point for this discourse analysis is the work of Boshier and Chia (1999), who identified four discourses: techno-utopianism, techno-cynicism, techno-zealotry, and techno-structuralism. These ideas may be regarded as polarising discourses in which the debates have become simplified into oppositional positions between the optimists who regard the Internet as a liberatory and empowering technology and the pessimists who warn of the exclusionary nature of the media and point to difficulties in ensuring mass access to the technologies (Webb, 1999). Empirical evidence can be found to support both positions, yet I would argue that if adult educators are to engage fully with these debates, the mechanisms by which this evidence is used to justify such diverse arguments needs to be examined. To answer this, the paper examines differences in the situations in which the Web has been used, because, as

157

others have argued, differences in the contexts and in the institutional purposes and players involved are critical to understanding how technologically based learning impacts on the participation of adult learners (Gorard and Selwyn, 1999; Webb, 1999).

Constructions of lifelong learning and web-based learning in recent UK policy

'The introduction of new technology into education has been a key component of [UK] government policy since around 1980' writes Somekh (2000:20) and initiatives have spanned schools, colleges, universities, public libraries, and more informal learning in community settings. These have included: the Superhighways programme (DfEE, 1995) the National Grid for Learning (DfEE, 1997), the Public Libraries Network; the University for Industry's (Ufi) 'learn direct' centres, college 'local learning hubs' which have been the Further Education Funding Council's response to the Learning Age document (DfEE, 1998), the New Opportunities Fund training for teachers and librarians, the National Lottery's Community Access to Lifelong Learning programme launched in 2000, digital colleges, such as the Welsh Coleg Digdol Cymru and e-university developments, and various higher education funding council initiatives such as Computers in Teaching (CTI) and the Teaching and Learning Technology project (TLTP). Not surprisingly, such a large scale investment in new technology has ensured that politicians and to some extent the enthusiastic innovators have high expectations that these initiatives will be transformative. Two themes have emerged. On the one hand there is an expectation that educational achievement will be increased, and in so doing, individuals and the country will accrue economic benefits, and on the other hand, the expansion of the class of the information rich will ensure that equity and social justice will prevail. In other words, underpinning these programmes are expectations of educational gains that will transform the economy and enhance social democracy. Techno-utopianism and techno-zealotry seem to dominate these accounts. Indeed, in some documents technological determinism seems to inform the arguments that information technology skills are a new form of literacy essential to a modern industrial democracy; information literacy is claimed to be a basic skill for lifelong learning (Ufi Learn Direct website); and a key skill for higher education (NCIHE, 1997).

The UK is not alone in encouraging these developments suggests Longworth (1999). Many governments are basing their strategies for more effective learning on the use of education technology, including open and distance learning and delivery through networks. The rationale for these developments is best summed up by a statement in the UK Government's Green Paper, 'The Learning Age', which argued that: 'As the University for Industry will demonstrate, one of the best ways to overcome some of the barriers to learning will be to use the new broadcasting and other technologies.' (DfEE, 1998, 1.2). Another aspect of the rationale is that the Ufi is expected to provide a structure of 'support for businesses to secure the skills that they need to compete in the world' by being a broker to stimulate employer-led training, and learning in the further and higher education sectors to address the UK's 'skills requirements and to improve UK competitiveness' (DfEE, 1998, 7.2).

What is interesting about these statements is that they infer two apparently different approaches to lifelong learning. On the one hand, the language positions the Ufi firmly within an inclusive discourse of lifelong learning that regards learning as essential for everyone to realise their individual human potential (Longworth, 1999). It proposes that this may be achieved by 'help[ing] all adults realise their potential by opening up access to learning through local opportunities, using technology, and broadcasting to create an open network' (DfEE, 1998, 1.2). In these ways, the language within The Learning Age articulates many of the key elements found within public narratives about social inclusion and widening participation, as the following claims about the use of new technologies illustrate: 'The Ufi will help people find the time to learn...make learning more accessible and affordable...provide a clear route to learning opportunities [and] take the fear out of learning' (DfEE, 1998, 9).

On the other hand, the policy document highlights a narrower conception of lifelong learning in which the Ufi is seen to be an instrumental mechanism to help solve the economic needs of the state and industry, and of individuals' needs for education and training to help their employment. A Skills Task Force is a central part of this strategy along with the setting of national education and training targets for everyone over 16 years of age (DfEE, 1998). Yet, as Robertson (1998) reminds us, this is a supply-sided initiative, rather than demand led and the focus is on what I described earlier as 'thin' access rather than 'thick' access. There is little evidence that those who have not traditionally participated in education and training will suddenly find this attractive, or that the content has been transformed, simply because it has been technologically 'repackaged' (Gorard and Selwyn, 1999).

A closer examination of the language and argument of the Learning Age (DfEE, 1998) document shows that it takes as its problem the underparticipation in formal education and training of certain sectors of the adult population and this is regarded as causally linked to institutional barriers (that is to the organisation of the provision) on the one hand, and to individual motivational or situational barriers (that is to an individual's fear, level of confidence and ability to afford, find the time or travel to the formal provision), on the other (see Cross, 1981; or McGivney, 1993 for a discussion of these barriers). It also presumes a link between levels of educational attainment and economic prosperity. In the extracts quoted above, typically the subjects of the sentences are the educational/training providers and businesses, the objects are adults with 'problems' who lack time, money, confidence or appropriate knowledge, and the verbs encourage action on the part of these providers to resolve these barriers or problems through ICT. Interestingly, the sentences also provide closed readings. Alternative explanations or outcomes are not suggested as the following highlighting of key words illustrates:

'best ways to **overcome** some of the **barriers** to learning will be to **use** the **new broadcasting and other technologies**' i.e. ICT solves access and participation barriers;

'[Ufi] support for **businesses** to secure the **[ICT] skills** that they **need to compete** in the world' i.e. ICT solves economic problems;

'help[ing] **adults** realise their **potential**' i.e. ICT solves problems of participation and encourages personal development;

'open up **access** to learning through **local opportunities**' i.e. ICT solves institutional barriers to access and participation;

'**help** people **find** the **time** to learn' i.e. ICT solves situational barriers to access and participation;

'be **accessible** and more **affordable**' i.e. ICT solves situational barriers to access and participation;

'provide a clear **route** to learning **opportunities**' i.e. ICT solves institutional barriers to access and participation;

'take the fear out of learning' i.e. ICT solves motivational barriers to access and participation.

In sum, the argument in this text links instrumental and economic conceptions of lifelong learning with public and private agendas of social inclusion, widening participation and personal growth and explanations of exclusion based on beliefs about motivational, situational and institutional barriers to education. One effect is to blur boundaries for the learner between learning for personal development and learning to get a better job. Underpinning these two approaches to lifelong learning is an optimistic account of the role of new learning technologies that invokes the discourses of techno-utopians and techno-zealots (Boshier and Chia, 1999) and their presence may explain why these two constructions of lifelong learning are not presented as a contradiction within these UK policies. In other words, the fluidity of the concept of lifelong learning has enabled policy makers to encompass on the one hand, the language of widening participation and social inclusion, albeit using a 'thin' rather than a 'thick' version of access, and on the other, appears to be addressing the economic needs of the state and industry.

However, if one adopts a politicised view of policy making, the rhetorical turn and extreme case formulation (Pomerantz, 1986) of these policy documents should not surprise. What is interesting though is how practitioner and researcher claims have echoed this theme of transformation. For example, for some it transforms the geography of lifelong learning by,

'removing some of the barriers of time, place and pace of learning which prevent adults from realising their learning potential' (Essom and Thomson, 1999:21).

In these accounts the focus shifts away from the formal educational institutions, the providers and their fixed and potentially inflexible locations and organisation, to the user and the flexible ways that learning can be experienced. Education has been redescribed as learning and the boundaries between formal and informal learning have become permeable in these conceptualisations of lifelong learning predicated on the information technology revolution.

...the information technology revolution is creating a new form of electronic, interactive education that should blossom into a lifelong learning system that allows almost anyone to learn almost anything from anywhere at any time. (Halal and Liebowitz, 1994:21)

Others claim that learning becomes less individualised and the technology and its use can encourage family learning, community learning and collaborative learning (Laurillard, 1993). Similarly, research accounts utilise the discourse of access and participation to highlight the role of information and communication technologies in overcoming 'individualised' motivational barriers (see Hardy et al 1994; McConnell, 1997; Sproull and Kiesler, 1993). They suggest that the apparent lack of social status cues in on-line interaction promotes social equality. In other words, these researchers and practitioners seem to be constructing a view of new technologies in education that identifies their transformative pedagogic potential which begins to shift the focus from 'thin' access to 'thick' access issues. Interestingly, some policy makers also appear to have reflected these arguments. For example, the Further Education Funding Agency's (1998) response to the Learning Age recommended that interaction between learners or other acknowledged experts will be essential to transform learning; Information Communication Technologies (ICT) will need to become Information Learning Technologies (ILT). Similarly, the Further Education Development Agency (1998:14) claimed that 'returning learners are excited by the new technology and can learn better with support...peer activity and a tutorial relationship'. More recently, Brown and Hunt (2000:16) also noted that 'at the Invitation Seminar on Technological Developments and the Ufi organised by the Ufi Transition Team in 1998 (TfT 1998), it was concluded that a tutorial element should be a significant element of the Ufi approach because dialogue is the essence of learning'.

It would seem therefore that UK policy documents and some researchers and practitioners have been constructing conceptualisations of lifelong learning which regard new technology as a tool for equity and social justice. These constructions align lifelong learning with widening participation debates and presume that there will be beneficial economic outcomes through an increase in educational attainment. In addition, the new technology is presumed to encourage different and more egalitarian or learner centred pedagogies in which knowledge is fluid rather than fixed. For some then, lifelong learning encourages greater social cohesion not merely through extending economic benefits to more people but through shifting models of learning from knowledge transfer and recall to social and personal construct models. An optimistic construction has emerged which aligns with the techno-utopianism and techno-zealotry of writers such as Rheingold (1994), who suggests that new global communities will develop that will replicate the spirit of efficacy of traditional societies, and cyber-feminists such as Haraway (1991), Plant (1996; 1997) and Turkle (1996), who have emphasised the radical possibilities for women posed by the 'soft mastery' forms of interaction and multiple identity constructions that the media facilitate. However, such discourses are contested.

The debates about web-based learning in reaching the learners who are hard to reach

There is a large and growing body of literature about the use of the Web in learning, about which a number of distinctions need to be drawn. These include firstly, recognising the use of technology for managing the teaching and learning process, where it may be used for marketing courses and institutions, providing information and guidance, registration, tracking, and assessment. Secondly, the use of computer mediated communications (CMC) such as e-mail, asynchronous conferencing, or synchronous conferencing. Thirdly, the use of the technology such as multi-user object orientated (MOOs) or multi user dimensions (MUDs) to simulate virtual environments. Inglis *et al* (1999) argue that each of these may draw on a range of pedagogic strategies. For example, they might include on the one hand, those that stress knowledge transfer, and emphasise the recall of set packages of knowledge; those that carefully sequence knowledge and encourage information transfer through structured teacher led activities; and those that encourage 'learning by doing' in order to achieve competency. On the other hand, there are others that see student to student and student to tutor interaction as critical to the students' learning, and these tend to draw on personal construction models, social construction models or conceptual shift models. It is the facility for these more interactive strategies that has given rise to a number of optimistic accounts of how Web learning may enhance adult learning, along with its apparent neutrality and public accessibility as a channel of information irrespective of time, place and institutional personnel.

For example, enthusiastic practitioners, who attempt to theorise the relationship between contexts, learning goals, learner characteristics and the learning media, in order to explore Internet learning and its value for adult learners, as in the case of Lyman's (1999) model of situated learning, provide accounts that accord with the discourses of techno-utopia and techno-zealot described earlier, but ones that are short on empirical evidence of adult learning. This is not surprising since much of the literature on computer mediated communications (CMC) has identified a tendency towards democratic interaction (Boyd, 1987; Harasim, 1987) and promoted a democratic theory about its use (Rheingold, 1994). It has suggested that the media lack social cues and this promotes social equality (Kiesler, 1987; Sproull and Kiesler, 1993). Further support has come from more recent studies of gender mixed on-line discussion groups (Hardy *et al*, 1994; McConnell, 1997; Selfe and Meyer, 1991). They have suggested that the communications technology, with its plain text format and the perceived ephemeralness of its messages, has led people to forget or ignore their audiences. They have argued that the medium contributes to deindividuation which means that the users of CMC become less sensitive to each other, and the resulting reduced social awareness leads to messages which ignore social boundaries, and involve greater levels of social revelation than in face to face encounters, which is why there is also more likely to be blunt 'speaking' or 'flaming' messages.

The debate is complex though, and most of the evidence marshalled to support arguments is based on work with traditional undergraduates, or post-graduates and those involved in continuing professional development. Nevertheless, some studies with more diverse and less traditional undergraduate groups that have been, for example, part-time, ethnically diverse or mature students, have suggested that de-individuation enhances disclosure and risk taking and increases personal construct learning (Chester and Gwynne, 1998), and self esteem (Alice, 1998; McCulley and Patterson, 1996). Indeed a review of North American literature by Kosakowski (1998) suggests information technology learning benefits the motivation, self confidence and esteem of students across all subjects when students are encouraged to develop control of their learning, but this is particularly the case when they are in at risk groups (such as special education, students from inner-city or rural schools). Similarly, there is some evidence that ICT is an effective learning media for the acquisition of basic skills when behaviourist models of learning are used to build confidence through reinforcement and learners can make mistakes in private (Kulik, 1994; Underwood and Brown, 1997). Some older and geographically isolated learners in Australia also have been found to value the opportunity to learn on-line (Swindell and Vassella, 1999).

However, these arguments are contested by techno-cynics and techno-structuralists (Boshier and Chia, 1999), and the table below suggests how this debate has been polarised around questions, such as, how does 'real life' interact with the virtual, and are there structural or dispositional constraints to learning on-line?

Table 1: Conceptualisations of the role of new technologies in learning (ICT)

Positive view	Negative view
Techno-utopians: 'ICTechnology is neutral'	Techno-cynics: 'ILTechnology use is social'
Techno-zealots: 'ICT is disembodied, fluid, free'	Techno-structuralists: 'ILT texts carry social markers'

The more negative accounts regard instances of de-individuation and flaming in on-line discussions, not as indicators that the technology is neutral, but rather that it is social and reflects for example, dominant masculine communication styles which inhibit women's participation (Tannen, 1991). In addition, these accounts are more likely to cite, as supporting evidence, data that highlights the gendered, aged and classed distribution of computer access and use (Balka, 1993; Thorpe, 2000) or ethnic differences (Richardson et al, 2000). More specifically, some writers have suggested that CMC does little to equalise differences in gendered communications, and may exacerbate some differences, even though some women's voices are increasingly being heard (Ferris, 1996; Herring, 1994; Pohl and Michaelson, 1998; We, 1993). In a similar way, others have shown that the Web carries social markers (Yates, 1997) and that as a different, but still social space, our understandings of how learning operates in different contexts and with different groups is as relevant to Internet and web-based learning as it is to the conventional classroom. The issue which underpins these concerns is the extent to which there are similarities and differences between CMC and face to face conversations. Studies which have explored this have argued that all communications' media are social constructs and that interaction is socially negotiated. Perrolle (1991) used Habermas' theory of linguistic competence to examine these matters and argued that because some of the social norms of communications such as how we build trust and develop linguistic competence are removed or obscured in CMC, there is the potential for communications via computers to be distorted. However, she also acknowledged that some social indicators of power and status differences which can negatively affect people's participation in face to face conversations can be hidden in CMC, and so there is a greater potential for more equal participation by each gender, class, race and ability group. In the end, Perrolle has been cautious in assuming that the technology will always be deployed in such emancipatory ways and has suggested that because the design and use of hardware and software is socially negotiated it may still reflect, and even reify, unequal relations of power and authority.

Equally problematic, for understanding how Web learning can be used to support lifelong learning and increase the participation of the socially excluded, is that much of the literature has been derived from studies of learners who have had considerable experience of formal education. For example, Paulsen (1994) has argued that it is the facility for 'many to many' communication techniques, more so than others, that gives Internet learning its major advantages over face to face learning,. However, Paulsen's samples involved well qualified learners and professional practitioners, and he offered little discussion of other factors which might have contributed to the success of the CMC. Similarly, Kaye (1992) recognised the relationships between the pedagogic style of the on-line tutor, and the potential of Web-based media to facilitate collaborative learning in his study of continuing professional development. Therefore, much of this literature originates from analyses of continuing professional development, and undergraduate and postgraduate teaching, and little seems to be changing (see for example Banks et al, 1998). Gorard and Selwyn's (1999) analysis of the virtual college movement in the UK concluded that educationalists and researchers should avoid viewing ICT as a 'technical fix' for post compulsory education and training. They suggest that one of the 'problems' of computers is that as Postman (1992) argues they encourage a focus on technical solutions, but this view obscures many of the social and cultural contexts of these new lifelong learning policies. Not surprisingly, these cases have contributed to the development of optimistic discourses about the use of Web-based learning, but little attention has been given to the impact of different settings, different educational purposes and differences among students.

Part of the reason for this lack of attention to the problem of meaning when constructing generalisations for policy and practice from diverse case studies may be because evaluations have frequently been practitioner-led (Inglis et al, 1999). Indeed, Somekh (2000) argues that this lack of independent evaluation has enabled policy-makers and the practitioners leading developments to selectively use the research literature to support their strategies and practices, and this has left many premises untested. Adopting this more realist approach to research data, Inglis et al (1999) have argued that the technology itself encourages innovation to keep ahead of the competition, and so, rather than wait for the results of longitudinal studies, policy is developed on the basis of the best understandings of known best practice.

They claim that even costings models tend to underestimate the full costs of development and delivery, and they suggest that technology cannot solve the access problems created by situational and institutional barriers. They argue that digital learning involving interaction between the tutor and the learner is probably no cheaper than face to face teaching. The main financial gains are likely to be felt by institutions that defray their high development costs through global marketing and recruitment of many small specialist groups of learners. In turn these learners who are seeking specialist professional provision gain access to learning that would otherwise be beyond their reach. Other benefits to institutions occur when they pass on the hidden costs of teaching and learning to students and staff who have to bear the additional costs of obtaining the equipment, line access, the materials, or acquire the skills to use the technology and find the time to set up systems and handle on-line material. Further cost benefits are most likely to accrue to those institutions where distance learning has used the remote classroom model rather than interactive learning, and these are more prevalent in the USA, than in Australia and the UK. If these findings are accepted they suggest that the recent UK strategies for lifelong learning centred on the Internet and the Web are based on some dubious assumptions about the costs and benefits to institutions and to disadvantaged individuals.

What can be concluded form this analysis? Evidence can be found to support both the positive and the negative conceptualisations of new technologies in learning. Protagonists from either perspective can assemble apparently robust arguments and find exemplars to fit their cases. For those that cling to wanting to know what is *really* going on, the literature is confusing. On the one hand, the use of interactive software enhances collaborative performance/ writing on-line for some groups under some circumstances, but we do not seem to know how such writing on-line relates to assessment and learning, nor how to answer the question will it work in my patch? (see for example, Lea's (2000) discussion of computer conferencing). The techno-structuralists argue that social differences that affect learning and participation are likely to spill-over into virtual environments not disappear, and so it is unlikely that the provision of local 'learning centres' will overcome the time and socio-economic costs for those individuals seeking access. Moreover, this provision tends to be narrowly skill based (Gorard and Selwyn, 1999). Home and workplace access may be increasing but other especially gender and class, differences of power and control over the use of equipment at home and work may emerge. Yet these more sceptical voices are silent in the policy documents that seek to align new technologies and widening participation agendas.

Conclusion

An alternative view of Internet and Web learning to that found in this policy discourse would be to regard the Internet as a medium that extends pre-existing identities and institutions rather than radically transforming them (Poster, 1997). This is neither an optimistic nor a pessimistic view of the technology but rather one that seeks to understand technology within a socially constructed context and to evaluate its use in diverse contexts, and in relation to learners and their goals. The argument of this paper has been that the majority of studies of on-line learning that have been associated with the optimistic discourses of the techno-utopianists and the techno-zealots have derived their findings from case studies within the field of continuing professional development and continuing vocational education or from work with traditional undergraduate and postgraduate university students. Few studies of on-line learning have focused on the non traditional learner or learners who have not participated beyond initial compulsory education.

In addition, many of the extrapolations from empirical research that have been used to make claims about the Web, have blurred different conceptualisations of lifelong learning, such as learning for personal development and promoting social inclusion, and learning to improve a country's competitiveness and enabling the individual to get a better job. The extent to which the Internet and web-based learning may be able to deliver these different objectives is likely to be variable and to some extent unknown. What is needed is a more extended analytical review of how different groups of adult learners interact on-line and perceive their learning. Analysis of a wider range of cases is likely to strengthen the argument that the context in which the Web is deployed has to be understood before one can assert that it will be the panacea for adult learning of the future and become a key strategy for educational activists and policy makers with a lifelong learning and widening participation agenda. Finally, my conclusion suggests that having examined the discursive practices that have led to the construction of the optimistic and pessimistic discourses of the Internet in learning I am advocating more '*real*' research. In part, this is the case, but I conclude by reminding readers that I am also an ICT enthusiast, and in this area of research exemplified by the case study, my practices and understandings are just as likely as others to be informed by 'naturalistic generalisations' (Stake, 1995:85) or discursive constructions rather than by dispassionate readings of so-called independent evaluations. Caution and reflexivity is therefore necessary when examining claims in this field.

References

Alice, L. (1996) 'Women's studies and the net effect' in *Feminist Collections*, 17 (2): 40-41.

Banks, S., and McConnell, D., (2000) 'Online learning using broadcast materials: a case study evaluation of the BBC on-line learning pilot programme in women's health', paper presented to the *Networked Lifelong Learning Conference 2000, University of Lancaster/University of Sheffield*.

Banks, S., Graebner, C., & McConnell, D. (1998) (eds) *Networked Lifelong Learning*. Sheffield: University of Sheffield.

Balka, E. (1993) 'Women's access to on-line discussions about feminism'. *Electronic Journal of Communication*, 3 (1).

Ball, S.J. (1990) *Policy and Policy Making in Education*, London: Routledge.

Boshier, R. W. (1999) Adult education adrift in a net: making waves or clutching a lifelong? *Proceedings of the 1999 annual Adult Education Research Conference*, http:www.edst.educ.ubc.ca/aerc/1999symp_boshier.

Boshier, R.W., & Chia, M.O. (1999) Discursive constructions of web learning and education: neither 'world wide' or open, *Proceedings of Pan-Commonwealth Forum Open Learning*. Universiti Brunei Darussalam and Commonwealth of Learning.

Boyd, G. (1987) Emancipative educational technology. *Canadian Journal of Educational Communication*, 16 (2) 167-172.

Brown, S., and Hunt. S., (2000) *Higher education and the Ufl, a regional perspective*. unpublished report for HEFCE.

Burbules, N.C. and Callister, T.A. Jr. (2000) *Watch IT, the risks and promises of information technologies for education*, Oxford: Westview Press.

Chester, A., and Gwynne, G. (1998) On-line teaching: encouraging collaboration through anonymity' in *Journal of Computer mediated Communications*, 4 (2) December 1998

Coffield, F. (1997) 'Introduction and overview: attempts to reclaim the concept of the learning society' in *Journal of Education Policy*, 12 (6) 449-455.

Cross, K.P., (1981) *Adults as Learners*, San Francisco: Jossey-Bass.

DfEE (1995) *Superhighways for Education*, London: Stationery Office.

DfEE (1997) *Connecting the Learning Society*, London: Stationery Office.

DfEE (1998) *The Learning Age: A Renaissance for a New Britain*, London: Stationery Office.

Edelman, M. (1977) *Political Language: Words that Succeed and Policies that Fail*. London: Academic Press.

Edwards, R. (1997) *Changing Places? Flexibility, Lifelong Learning and a Learning Society.* London: Routledge.

Essom, J. and Thomson, A. (1999) 'All mapped out', in *Adults Learning*, 11 (3) 21-22

Ferris, S.P. (1996) Women on-line: cultural and relational aspects of women's communication in on-line discussion groups. *Interpersonal Computing and Technology: An Electronic Journal for the 21st Century*, 4 (3-4) 29-40. http://www.helsinki.fi/science/optek/1996n3/ferris.txt.

Further Education Development Agency (1998) *The Learning Age: FEDA's Response.* London: FEDA.

Further Education Funding Council (1998) *Response to the Government's Green Paper, 'The Learning Age' by FEFC's Further Education Information and Learning Technology Committee*, Coventry: FEFC.

Gorard, S. & Selwyn, N. (1999) Switching on the Learning Society? Questioning the role of technology in widening participation and lifelong learning. *Journal of Education Policy*, 14.

Halal, W.E. & Liebowitz, J. (1994) Telelearning: the multimedia revolution in education. *The Futurist* Nov-Dec, 21-26.

Harasim, L. (1987) Teaching and learning online: issues in computer mediated graduate courses. *Canadian Journal of Educational Communication*, 16 (2) 117-135.

Haraway, D. (1991) *Simians, Cyborgs and Women. The Reinvention of Nature.* London: Free Association Books.

Hardy, V., Hodgson, V., & McConnell, D. (1994) Computer conferencing: a new medium for investigating issues in gender and learning. *Higher Education*, 28, 403-418.

Herring, S. (1994) Gender differences in computer mediated communication: bringing familiar baggage to the new frontier. Proceedings of *American Library Association Annual Convention*, Miami, http://www.inform-umd.edu/EdRes/Topic/Womens.Studies.

HEFCE (1999) News, 10 February 1999, HEFCE website http://www.HEFCE.ac.uk

NCIHE (1997) *National Committee of Inquiry into Higher Education, Higher Education for the 21st Century*, London: Stationery Office.

Inglis, A., Ling, P., & Joosten, V. (1999) *Delivering Digitally*, London: Kogan Page.

Jarvis, P. (2000) Lifelong learning- an agenda for a late modern future, *in Post Compulsory Education and the new Millennium*, ed. D.E. Gray and C. Griffen, London: Jessica Kingsley publications.

Kaye, A.R. (1992) Learning together apart, in A. R. Kaye (ed.) *Collaborative Learning Through Computer Conferencing*, (The Najaden Papers) Berlin: Springer-Verlag.

Kiesler, S. (1987) Social aspects of computer environments, *Social Science*, 72, 23-28.

Kosakowski, J., (1998) 'The benefits of Information Technology' Eric Digest (on-line) www.ericit.syr.edu/ithome/digests/edoir9804.html

Kulik, J.A. (1994) 'Meta-analytic studies of findings on computer based instruction', in E.L.Baker and H.F. O'Neil, Jr. (eds.) *Technology Assessment in Education and Training*, Hillsdale, NJ: Lawrence Erlbaum.

Laurillard, D. (1993) *Rethinking University Teaching: a Framework for the Effective Use of Educational Technology*, London: Routledge.

Lea, M. (2000) 'Computer conferencing: new possibilities for writing and learning in higher education', in Lea, M. and Stierer, B. (eds) *Student Writing in Higher Education -new contexts*, Milton Keynes: Open University Press/ SRHE

Longworth, N. (1999) *Making Lifelong Learning Work*, London: Kogan Page.

Lyman, B. (1999) Internet-based learning: what's in It for the adult learner? In D. French, C. Hale, C. Johnson, & G. Farr (eds) *Internet-based Learning*, London: Kogan Page.

Lyotard, J-F. (1984) *The Postmodern Condition*, Manchester: Manchester University Press.

McConnell, D. (1997) Interaction patterns of mixed sex groups in educational computer conferences. Part 1 - Empirical findings. *Gender and Education* 9 (3), 345-363.

McConnell, D. (1998) Developing networked learning professionals: a critical perspective. in S. Banks, C. Greabner & D. McConnell, (eds) *Networked Lifelong Learning* Sheffield: University of Sheffield.

McCulley, L. and Patterson, P. 'Feminist empowerment through the Internet' in *Feminist Collections*, 17 (2) pp 5-6.

McGivney,V. (1993) *Women, Education and Training. Barriers to access, informal starting points and progression routes*. Leicester, NIACE.

Nicoll, K. (1999) 'Troubling spaces in the analysis of adult education policy' in *Proceedings of 29th annual conference of SCUTREA* ed. B. Merrill, Warwick: University of Warwick.

Paulsen, M. F. (1994) Some pedagogical techniques for computer mediated communication. In M. F. Verdejo and S. A. Cerri, (eds), *Collaborative Dialogue Technologies in Distance Learning*, London: Springer-Verlag.

Perrolle, J. A. (1991) Conversations and trust in computer interfaces. In C. Dunlop & R. Kling (eds) *Computerization and Controversy: Value Conflicts and Social Choices*, Boston: Academic Press Inc.

Plant, S. (1996) 'On the matrix: cyberfeminist simulations', in Shields, R. (ed.) *Cultures of Internet*, London: Sage.

Plant, S. (1997) *Zeros and Ones*. London: Fourth Estate.

Pohl, M. & Michaelson, G. (1998) "I don't think that's an interesting dialogue": Computer-mediated communication and gender, in A.F. Grundy, D. Kohler, V. Oechtering, & V. Peterson, (eds) *Women, Work and Computerisation*, Berlin: Springer.

Pomerantz, A. (1986) 'Extreme case formulations: A way of legitimising claims' in *Human Studies* 9:219-229.

Poster, M (1992) *The mode of Information*, London: Polity Press.

Postman, N. (1992) *Technopoly: the Surrender of Culture to Technology*. New York:Vintage Books.

Rheingold, H. (1994) *The Virtual Community*, London: Secker and Warburg.

Richardson, J., Norfles, N., Green, P. and Yeakey, C. (2000) 'Higher education in a global economy: an evaluation of critical issues in post-secondary institutions in the United States' paper presented to EAN Annual Convention 2000, Santiago de Compostela, Spain.

Robertson, D. (1998) The University for Industry: a flagship for demand-led training or another doomed supply-side intervention? *Journal of Education and Work*, 11, (1).5-22.

Selfe, C. & Meyer, P. R. (1991) Testing claims for on-line conferences, *Written Communication*, 8, 162-192.

Somekh, B. (2000) 'New technology and learning policy: policy and practice in the UK, 1980 - 2010', in *Education and Information Technologies*, 5:1 (2000): 19-35.

Sproull, L. & Kiesler, S. (1993) *Connections: New Ways of Working in the Networked Organization*. Cambridge Mass.: The MIT Press.

Stake, R. (1995) *The Art of Case Study Research*, London: Sage.

Strain, M. and Field, J. (1997) 'On the myth of the learning society', *British Journal of Educational Studies*, 45 (2), 144-155.

Swindell, R. and Vassella, K. (1999) *Older Learners Online: An Evaluation of Internet Courses for Isolated Older Persons*. Nathan, Brisbane:Griffiths University.

Tannen, D. (1991) *You just don't understand*. London: Virago.

Thorpe, M. (2000) New technology and lifelong learning, Open University Lifelong Learning on-line seminar, summer 2000, www.ou.ac.uk.

Turkle, S. (1995) *Life on Screen: Identity in the Age of the Internet*, New York: Simon and Shuster.

Underwood, J., and Brown, J. (eds.) (1997) *Integrated Learning Systems, Potential into Practice*, Oxford: Heinemann.

Usher, R. and Edwards, R. (1994) *Postmodernism and Education:Different Voices, Different Worlds*, London: Routledge.

We, G. (1993) *Cross-gender communication in cyberspace*. unpublished ms. Simon Fraser University.

Webb, S. (1999) Understanding meanings of distance in face to face and on-line learning, *Proceedings of 29th annual conference of SCUTREA*, ed. B. Merrill, Warwick: University of Warwick.

Weiss, C. and Bucuvalas, M. (1980) *Social Science Research and Decision Making*, New York; Columbia University Press.

Wiseman, M., and Kendall, S. (2000) 'Providing a framework for the evaluation of e-technology implementation to widen participation in higher education' paper presented to *EAN Annual Convention 2000*, Santiago de Compostela, Spain.

Yates, S. (1997) Gender, identity and CMC, *Journal of Computer Assisted Learning*, 13, 281-290.

Chapter Thirteen

Developing an evaluation framework: assessing the contribution of community-based and work-based approaches to lifelong learning amongst educationally marginalised adults

Liz Thomas and Kim Slack

Introduction

Throughout Europe lifelong learning is a growing phenomenon, that has the *potential* to pay social dividends. This is discussed more fully elsewhere.

> 'Education and training are often perceived as a counter to social exclusion in that they facilitate social 'networking', develop self-confidence and enhance labour market participation' (Thomas and Jones, 2000, p8).

Despite this potential, the emphasis of policy and especially implementation, is on the economic benefits of lifelong learning at the expense of socially excluded groups (see Woodrow *et al*, 2000). It is therefore necessary to develop appropriate ways of reaching educationally marginalised groups, and of evaluating the effectiveness of such initiatives.

This chapter examines two case studies of strategies to promote lifelong learning amongst adults who have not previously participated in post-compulsory formal learning. One is a community-based initiative involving further education colleges and community link workers. This project targets adults and offers community-based courses. The second case study is a work-based scheme, offering NVQs (National Vocational Qualifications assessed via a portfolio of work demonstrating competencies) to non-teaching staff in schools. These staff are primarily parents (women), often described as the 'mum's army', who are employed in part-time, low-paid work as lunch time supervisors and learning support assistants (LSAs) or classroom assistants and who would not otherwise be participating in lifelong learning. A grounded theory approach has been used to analyse each case study and is then used to compare community-based and work-based approaches to lifelong learning to promote social inclusion. The grounded theory approach is then used to conceptualise a framework to evaluate widening participation initiatives orientated towards promoting lifelong learning amongst educationally marginalised adults. This chapter presents a substantive theory of evaluation that can be applied empirically by other practitioners to evaluate their work and contribute towards a formal theory of evaluation.

Case study 1: using a 'strategic partnership' to promote participation in lifelong learning in excluded communities

This case study focuses on an example of community-based learning that sought to widen participation in lifelong learning amongst educationally marginalised adults. The initiative was a 'strategic partnership', as proposed by the Kennedy Committee in the report *Learning Works* (Kennedy, 1997). The aim of strategic partnerships was to bring together key local agencies in regions to collaborate to plan and deliver strategies together to widen participation amongst disadvantaged groups (see Kennedy, 1997 and FEDA, 1998).

Strategic partnerships were intended to overcome some of the limitations of competition in the further education sector, which had been introduced by the 1992 Further and Higher Education Act. Kennedy noted that this had '...*encouraged colleges not just to be businesslike but to perform as if they were businesses*', (Kennedy *et al,* p3). It was acknowledged that recruiting and retaining non-traditional learners is more costly than traditional students, and businesses tend not to undertake less profitable activities. For lifelong learning to promote equality, currently under-represented groups need opportunities to participate in education and learning.

Overview of the Strategic Partnership

The Partnership itself consisted of a range of collaborating agencies, but the primary partners were the eight further education colleges within one county. Each college received funding to employ (on a part-time basis) one Education Community Link-worker. As the job title suggests the link-workers' task was to serve as a conduit between the community and the college. Each college used post-code analysis (see Tonks, 1999) to identify localities with particularly low rates of participation in further education to select a 'target community'. Consolidating (or forging) contacts with individuals and groups in these areas, the link-workers' role was to help prospective students to overcome cultural and structural barriers to participation in further education.

The initial intention, as proposed in the bid submitted to the FEFC, was for each college to recruit a link-worker from the specified locale as previous pilot work suggested that:

'...people drawn from the community are most successful in working with that community and find successful solutions in increasing participation.'

A further feature of the project was an Open College Network (OCN) level two qualification undertaken by each link-worker. This was designed to address three areas of link-workers' work: the purpose and requirements of their role; methods and means of communication with selected communities; and possible ways to overcome barriers to learning. This course also gave link-workers first-hand experience of undertaking an OCN course, which was seen to be advantageous as many courses potential students consider enrolling on are accredited by the OCN. The course assessment required each link-worker to produce a portfolio-handbook of their work relating to community development and learning in the post-compulsory sector, to demonstrate pre-determined competencies.

Who did it target?

The geographic boundaries of the target communities were clear to all members of the partnership, but particularly at the start of the initiative, link-workers, and their managers, were not aware of designated socio-cultural groups within these locations that they should be targeting. In the early stages of the scheme link-workers named the following as possible target groups: lone parents, unemployed people, people on low incomes, working class people, people without qualifications, people who lack basic skills, people who lack motivation, ethnic and religious groups, people aged 18-25 years, and middle class women. This disparate list of potential entrants is not based on any formal research or analysis by the link-workers or their managers

As the initiative progressed many of the link-workers did not really tighten the focus of their efforts, but they adopted a pragmatic approach, often working with established groups, and whichever ones would co-operate with them. One link-worker explained:

'I found, because of lack of time, that I have gone to already established groups. I've actually been to young mums and I've been to older people – like luncheon clubs. But I also made sure I included unemployed men by going to the Job Centre'.

What did link-workers do?

The role of link workers was not rigidly defined. In broad terms, link-workers were facilitators or sources of encouragement to potential entrants; a press release described them as 'the voice of the college in the community and the voice of the community in the college'. In some ways they 'personalised' the potentially faceless bureaucratic arm of institutional recruitment, and helped to overcome recalcitrance of the target communities with regard to participating in lifelong learning. One link-worker commented that:

> 'the community thinks that the college is … not someone they can talk to on an equal level….. (and is seen as) too high and mighty … A lot of people (in the community) think of college as the same as school and many …. have bad memories of school'.

Their line manager, a project co-ordinator and the OCN course supported link-workers with the development and implementation of their role. The evaluation research (Thomas *et al*, 1999) found that link-workers undertook a wide range of tasks that can be categorised as establishing and developing contacts, assessing learners' needs, and course provision.

(i) Establishing and developing contacts

Link-workers developed two primary approaches to link working, which were identified in the evaluation research (*ibid*). These were 'networking' with agencies and 'one-to-one contacts' with individuals.

'Networking' involved making links with other organisations operating in the area, either to directly gain access to groups of potential students, or to seek referrals. Link-workers aimed to establish themselves as a point of referral so that each group would know whom to contact if a group member or a client had an interest in education. Link-workers liased with voluntary organisations, religious groups, public sector agencies and regeneration initiatives. The extent of referrals from other organisations was less than anticipated, but schools were cited as the most productive referral points, especially when courses were then delivered in a local school base. Not all link-workers found networking productive, indeed, one link-worker reported: 'I'm wasting a lot of time talking to agencies and not getting out there in the community.'

One positive benefit of networking was that this enabled some link-workers to establish a physical base in the community shared with colleagues from other agencies, allowing community members to approach link-workers directly. Without prior links with other agencies it is doubtful that this situation would have arisen. One link-worker felt that she was unable to encourage potential entrants onto courses due to the absence of a place at which she could be contacted at specified times; she asked: 'how can I have one-to-ones with nowhere to go?'.

Link-workers recruited from the target communities prioritised 'one-to-one' contact with potential entrants. It was anticipated that local link-workers would be familiar with the locale and its inhabitants, which would facilitate trust, contact and eventually participation in lifelong learning. Link-workers from the target community appeared to have less difficulty breaking down some of the barriers that other link-workers experienced, for example, one link-worker commented how she had to be prepared to deal with inquiries at all times. She wrote 'people are stopping me in the streets to ask about the courses. I carry information about with me everywhere, even collecting my children or going to the shops.'

(ii) Assessing learners' needs

Both the Kennedy Report (1997) and the Further Education Funding Council (FEFC, 1997a and 1997b) allure to the necessity to 'identify the learning needs of these groups' (FEFC, 1997b, p13). Indeed, some link-workers did attempt to find out what the learning needs or wants of the communities they were working with were, and they devised their own methods to achieve this goal. In particular, they utilised questionnaires with members of the target group and with employers, but the return rate was generally low, and thus link-workers resorted to more informal approaches to 'identifying and assessing need', such as relying on individuals meeting them to discuss their needs, and agency referrals. There was not therefore a systematic assessment of the learning needs of the geographical communities targeted by this initiative.

(iii) Course provision

Link-workers often become involved in operational matters relating to course provision, for example, identifying suitable locations, enrolling students, collecting course fees and overcoming organisational difficulties. This was facilitated or hindered by both the structure and the culture of the institutions concerned. In particular, the extent to which colleges were willing to respond to the needs of alternative learners was determined by attitudes and the institutional culture, and the flexibility that enabled colleges to meet the needs of different learning groups was determined by the organisational structure.

Outcomes of the initiative

There was debate within the partnership regarding how success should be assessed, and both qualitative and quantitative indicators were utilised.

Community awareness and attitudes towards education

Awareness of lifelong learning was raised by the project. Link-workers established a 'presence' in the community, often by providing a drop-in service, plus other activities and events (e.g. a community fun day and visits by the Jobs Bus). Link-workers reported a growth in positive attitudes, both towards themselves and education in general, (although formal measurement of attitudes was not undertaken). Comments such as this were common:

'I think I've increased information about education within the community. I've raised awareness of education ...I've raised people's awareness that these things are available'.

Course enrolments

Analysis of course enrolments found that participation in formal learning had increased in most of the geographical areas during the first ten months of the partnership. This however ranged from a net gain of ten students, to an increase of 109 students from one area, and percentage increases ranged from 2% to 28%. It is difficult to reach conclusions from this data, as the number of geographical areas, the size of each area, the number of other initiatives in each area, the initial participation levels and other factors all varied between the target geographical communities.

Progression

Link-workers all reported increased confidence amongst course participants, and this was often demonstrated by the desire of whole cohorts to progress to other courses. In the early stages most progression was to similar provision, for example other short leisure courses.

Unintended outcomes – new opportunities

Some outcomes of the initiative were unexpected. An interesting example was of a group of students who attended a ' painting on glass' leisure course, and subsequently started-up a small business.

The development of co-operation between colleges and other agencies

Further positive outcomes of the programme were the development of co-operation between participating institutions. Links were forged at the senior management level and between practitioners.

With very small financial inputs this programme clearly benefited the targeted communities, but the short-time scale of the initial funding was a limiting factor. Furthermore, link-workers faced 'internal' and 'external' barriers. Internal barriers included not being familiar with institutional procedures and college bureaucracy associated with responding to the needs of the target communities. External barriers included cultural/communication issues – overcoming entrenched perceptions of learning was a slow process, and relationships with other agencies were sometimes problematic.

Case Study 2: Work-based learning for non-teaching 'low status' staff in schools

This case study focuses on the introduction of a work-based scheme in schools offering lunch time supervisors and classroom assistants the opportunity to study for NVQs in Playwork, Learning and Development and Child Care and Education (now superseded by Early Years Care and Education). These staff, primarily women, are often described as the 'mums' army' and accorded relatively low status within school.

The scheme was implemented by Staffordshire County Council Quality Learning Services (QLS) three years ago. QLS is the inspection and support unit of the Local Education Authority and a provider of a range of programmes leading to National Vocational Qualifications, in particular Playwork and Early Years Care and Education qualifications, recommended for adults working as learning support assistants and lunchtime supervisors in schools. Their work in this area was stimulated by the desire to recognise the valuable contribution made by support staff within schools to the learning and development of young people. Such staff may not always have had access to professional development opportunities or nationally recognised accreditation, a fact acknowledged by both support staff themselves and head teachers.

The initial aim of the scheme, to impact on school improvement, was based on the premise that improving the whole school environment would have a beneficial effect on pupil's attitudes towards school and learning. The idea originated from a member of QLS staff who saw the potential of NVQs to allow support staff to have their experiential knowledge accredited. Ideally, this would raise levels of skill within the school enabling more effective and efficient operation. Concurrent with this was the assumption that completion of an NVQ would raise self-esteem amongst participants and that this would feed back into the school environment and ultimately benefit pupils. This assertion is supported by research (c.f. George 1994, Callender *et al.* 1993) which suggests that NVQs not only validate low status work but provide, what Issitt calls a 'value-added' component (Issitt 1996). In other words NVQs have 'value-added' in not only accrediting performance in the workplace, but also enhancing self-esteem and perceived competence at the personal level. Importantly, the scheme also provides a potential model for promoting lifelong learning within the school and work environment.

It is widely agreed that schools should aim to nurture a habit of lifelong learning in young people, and furthermore should embrace all members of the school community as both contributors to and participants in the learning environment. But does this extend to adults as well as children, non-teaching as well as teaching staff? Unfortunately, in many instances this does not seem to be the case in that '... *most schools are not yet places where adults as well as children are encouraged to learn'* (Day 1999, p.202). QLS encourage support staff in both primary and secondary schools to take part in the NVQ scheme. This not only provides an opportunity for professional development but it is also intended to recognise the valuable contribution that support staff make to the lives of pupils and the school in general. Support work is commonly regarded as low status, staff are thought of as amateur, just 'mums helping out'. By promoting professional development amongst support staff the local authority has played a key role in helping to promote lifelong learning in schools amongst a 'neglected audience', staff who are often accorded low status but who in fact play a central role in the lives of many school children.

Overview of the scheme

As an introduction to the scheme, QLS hold awareness raising sessions two or three times per year. Successful candidates from previous intakes contribute to these sessions. In principle, school support staff attend an awareness raising session, return to school and involve the head teacher who then contacts other schools, and ultimately a group is formed of people interested in participating in an NVQ course. This group subsequently takes part in an induction session held by QLS in a local school. For staff who subsequently become involved in the scheme, further instruction is then based around locally-held tutorials with cluster groups of participants, designed to share, develop and relate practice to National Standards. One-to-one sessions and workshops also take place, ultimately designed to assist participants to build a portfolio of evidence demonstrating that they have the requisite competency level.

Although a number of operational teething problems were apparent in the initial evaluation, the QLS Vocational Education team is currently working to overcome these. For example, they now provide detailed guidance for their NVQ programmes, (which includes a 'jargon buster'), together with full resource materials available as and when required, allowing participants to structure their own learning and evidence collection. Many participants, however, find working in cluster groups beneficial in terms of mutual support and the pooling of ideas.

Participation in the scheme

Motivation and responsibility for involvement in the scheme has come from both participants themselves and the senior school staff. Some support staff have taken the first step themselves, feeling that it is important in terms of their professional standing to gain a qualification validating the work they are doing within school. Few of the participants hold post-16 qualifications, for many the scheme represents their first experience of formal learning since leaving school. Where the impetus for participation in the scheme has come from senior school staff (i.e. the head teacher or the special education needs co-ordinator) this has been for one of two reasons. Firstly, there is recognition of the need for a universal qualification in respect of Learning Support Assistants. Secondly, in one school in particular the head teacher held a strong commitment to the concept of professional development for non-teaching, as well as teaching staff.

Outcomes

The source of the initial impetus has significant bearing on the outcomes of the scheme. Support from the head teacher, as suggested by previous research, is fundamental to the success of the scheme (Day 1999 and Eraut et al. 1997a). QLS also aim to recruit assessors in schools who will achieve their qualification alongside the first cohort of candidates, and then assess/mentor subsequent cohorts.

Support staff operate within the setting of their own school, their role is defined by the culture of the school that they work in. If the school environment is receptive to the development of non-teaching staff and they are allowed to contribute and thereby expand their role, they report higher levels of satisfaction and self-esteem following completion of the scheme.

In schools where the culture is less receptive, feelings of frustration are evident, described by one LSA as '*the more we have got on this course the more we have felt confined*'. Conflict has arisen over differing perceptions of the role of support staff within the school. Concern has been expressed by some teaching staff that the roles of teachers and learning support assistants have become blurred, the role of the latter becoming 'inflated' or exaggerated. Similarly, if support staff feel they lack respect and professional status within school, their potential (and that of the scheme) is curtailed.

The issues involved therefore are clearly complex. By expecting more from support staff in terms of qualifications and encouraging professional development, they may in turn expect more from employers in terms of pay and responsibility. Alternatively if recognition is not given in either of these areas, support staff feel frustrated and disheartened, and are unlikely to pursue further educational opportunities. For many of the staff involved in the scheme, the course represents a return to learning, if not their first such experience, then the most intensive since leaving school. Many of the participants in the scheme felt that it was important to carry on learning in some form, and valued qualifications not only in terms of employment, but also as a personal achievement relating to feelings of self-worth and value. Importantly this motivation was for some now coupled with an increased confidence in their own ability to undertake further study. With positive reinforcement from both teaching and non-teaching staff within the school, embarking on an NVQ may be the first crucial step towards lifelong learning.

Comparisons and the mode of analysis

These two case studies have been chosen because they both seek to engage with adults who have been effectively marginalised from the post-compulsory education sector. Furthermore, each case study has a particular approach to promoting lifelong learning (i.e. community-based and work-based learning), but which has been implemented by different institutions (i.e. colleges and schools), thus enabling comparisons to be made between a range of examples.

This is particularly important as the primary mode of analysis that has informed this paper is grounded theory (drawing from the work of Glaser & Strauss, 1967 and Strauss & Corbin, 1990), which is dependent on the comparison of cases. In answer to the question 'what is a grounded theory?' Strauss and Corbin supply the following explanation:

'A grounded theory is one that is inductively derived from the study of the phenomenon it represents. That is, it is discovered, developed, and provisionally verified through systematic data collection and analysis of data pertaining to that phenomenon. Therefore, data collection, analysis, and theory stand in reciprocal relationship with each other. One does not begin with a theory, then prove it. Rather, one begins with an area of study and what is relevant to that area is allowed to emerge' (Strauss and Corbin, 1990, p23).

The aim has been to use the comparisons of the case studies and the different implementing institutions within a grounded theory approach to conceptualise a framework to evaluate 'tailored initiatives' aimed at widening participation and promoting lifelong learning amongst educationally marginalised adults.

The choice of grounded theory is firstly because it produces research that is 'of use to professionals or lay audiences' (*ibid* p25), in other words it is of value to practitioners as well as academics. It is considered to be important by the authors to 'establish a relationship with both practitioners and researchers' (Jary & Thomas, 1999, p7), and thus 'a key role of research into access and lifelong learning should be to generate useful knowledge and to inform and assist others' (*ibid*). (See also Thomas and Jones, 2000b). The second, related, issue is that grounded theory does not impose a top-down evaluation framework, which may be inappropriate and ineffective. This is in keeping with the authors' view of the role of evaluation of widening participation initiatives (c.f. Thomas, 2000).

Comparisons and the conceptualisation of an evaluation framework

This section of the paper utilises comparisons between the two case studies and between implementation in particular institutions to conceptualise an evaluation framework for, what we have termed 'tailored initiatives' for 'educationally marginalised' adults. Six evaluation categories, or 'topics', have been developed: targeting; reaching new learners and identifying their needs; meeting the needs of new learners; student development and progression; sustainability and generalisability. Each of these categories includes a number of subcategories.

All the subcategories have been framed as questions, thus enabling them to be used as evaluation criteria. The evaluation topics and questions are presented in Table 1, together with a very brief evaluation of the community-based and the work-based learning case studies, plus general comments.

Table 1: Evaluation framework for lifelong learning 'tailored initiatives' for 'educationally marginalised' adults: a comparison between community-based and work-based approaches

Evaluation Topics	Evaluation Questions
1. Targeting	1.1 Who is targeted? 1.2 Is the target population educationally marginalised? 1.3 Is targeting effective?
2 Reaching new learners and identifying their needs	2.1 Is awareness of learning opportunities raised? 2.2 Are new learning needs identified? 2.3 Do the providers elicit what the learners' needs are?
3 Meeting the needs of new learners: are 'providers' flexible with respect to meeting learners' needs?	3.1 Are appropriate courses/activities provided (including a relevant curriculum)? Control or empowerment? 3.2 Are courses/activities in accessible locations and at convenient times? 3.3 Are support services (e.g. childcare, guidance etc) available?
4 Student development and opportunities for progression	4.1 Are students encouraged and able to progress (horizontal and/or vertically)? 4.2 Is personal development promoted? 4.3 Is social cohesion promoted? 4.4 Does learning/activities improve ability/opportunities in current employment? 4.5 Does the learning/activities improve employment prospects?
5 Sustainability	5.1 Is the scheme financially sustainable? 5.2 What will remain beyond the initial funding period? 5.3 Is the capacity of the participant group(s) developed? 5.4 Who owns the initiative? 5.5 Does organisational learning take place?
6 Generalisability	6.1 Is the scheme replicable? 6.2 What are the limitations?

Conclusion

This article has compared and contrasted two alternative approaches to promoting lifelong learning amongst educationally marginalised adults. The aim is not to pass a final judgement and conclude which method is the 'best', but to develop an evaluation framework. The evaluation topics (categories) and questions (subcategories) presented in Table 1 have been inducted using a grounded theory approach from the empirical research presented in these two case studies. This mode of analysis has proved to be a useful method of generating an evaluation framework to compare and contrast these two case studies. But more importantly, both researchers and practitioners can use this tool to evaluate other tailored initiatives that aim to widen participation in lifelong learning amongst educationally marginalised adults.

References

Callender, C., Toye., Connor, H. & Spilsbury, M. (1993) *National Vocational Qualifications: Early indications of employers' take-up and use*. Brighton, Institute of Manpower Studies.

Day, C. (1999) *Developing teachers: The challenges for lifelong learning*. London, Falmer Press.

Eraut, M., Alderton, J., Cole, G. & Senker, P. (1997a) 'Learning from other people at work' in Coffield, F. (ed) *Skill Formation*. Bristol, Policy Press.

FEDA (1998) *Programme: First Lesson for the Widening Participation Strategic Partnership*. Conference held 18th November 1998. London: Further Education Development Agency.

FEFC (1997a) *How to Widen Participation – A Guide to Good Practice*. Coventry: FEFC

FEFC (1997b) *Identifying and Addressing Needs*. Coventry: FEFC.

George, M. (1994) 'The first rung.' in *Community Care*, 17th Feb.

Glaser, B. and Strauss, A. (1967) *The Discovery of Grounded Theory*. Chicago, Aldine.

Issitt, M. (1996) *Competence in the Quasi-Market: Towards the Development of a Feminist Critique*. Housing and Community Research Unit, Staffordshire University.

Jary, D. and Thomas, E. (1999) 'Widening participation and lifelong learning. Rhetoric or reality? The role of research and the reflexive practitioner' in *Widening Participation and Lifelong Learning*, 1.1 pp3-9.

Kennedy, H. (1997) *Learning Works – widening participation in further education*. Coventry: FEFC.

OECD (1999) *Overcoming Exclusion Through Adult Learning*. Paris: OECD.

Slack, K. (1999) 'Lifelong learning in schools: qualifications for non-teaching staff' in *Journal of Widening Participation and Lifelong Learning* 1(2):44-46.

Strauss, A. and Corbin, J. (1990) *Basics of Qualitative Research. Grounded Theory Procedures and Techniques*. Newbury Park, California, Sage Publications.

Thomas, E. (2000) '"Bums on Seats" or "Listening to Voices": Evaluating widening participation initiatives using a PAR Approach' in *Studies in Continuing Education*.

Thomas, E. and Jones, R. (2000a) 'Social exclusion and higher education' in Thomas, E. and Cooper, M. (eds) *Changing the Culture of the Campus: Towards an inclusive higher education*. Stoke on Trent: Staffordshire University Press.

Thomas, E. and Jones, R. (2000b) 'Policy, practice and theory: the role of higher education research in combating social exclusion' in Thomas, E. and Cooper, M. (eds) *Changing the Culture of the Campus: Towards an inclusive higher education*. Stoke on Trent: Staffordshire University Press.

Thomas, E., Jones, R., Johnson, M. and Spencer, P. (1999) *Staffordshire Strategic Partnership Evaluation Report*. Stafford: Stafford College.

Thomas, E. and Slack, K. (1999) *Staffordshire Quality Learning Service NVQ Scheme: An evaluation of the perceived impact of work-based learning for support staff in schools*. Stoke-on-Trent, Institute for Access Studies, Staffordshire University

Tonks, D. (1999) 'Access to UK higher education, 1991-98: using geodemographics' in *Widening Participation and Lifelong Learning*, 1.2, p6-15

Woodrow, M., Feutrie, M., Grieb, I., Staunton, D. and Tuomisto, J. (2000) 'Lifelong learning to combat social exclusion: policies, provision and participants in five European countries', in *Widening Participation and Lifelong Learning*, 2.2, pp6-17.

Chapter Fourteen

Empowering the disadvantaged: how students from non-traditional backgrounds became leaders in student politics

Derek Bland

Introduction

Every year during the Q-Step Programme orientation at Queensland University of Technology (QUT), commencing students are encouraged to become fully involved in all that the University can offer including the clubs, societies and politics that help make up the total student experience. Until this year, however, the participation of Q-Step students in mainstream student politics has been peripheral, with one notable exception. This situation is not particularly surprising as students who enter the University through the Q-Step Programme are from socio-economically disadvantaged backgrounds and are, as such, very much a minority group within the university. What is surprising is that during 1999, a group of five Q-Step students collaborated in a team that won the elections for the QUT Student Guild (union) and took up office in a variety of executive positions. From these positions, they are now having some impact on the development of the University.

What motivates and enables students to become student leaders and devote much of their very valuable time to organising and implementing activities additional to their studies, jobs and private lives? In a far-reaching literature search, Silver and Silver (1997: 9) lament the lack of information, other than anecdotal, on 'the campus lives of students – for example, their willingness and ability to stand for union office.' They point out that, at least in Britain, student union records and papers are treated as dispensable ephemera with no research advantage taken of them or the experience of student officers. Australia's situation appears to be similar.

In a paper delivered to Australia's first National Conference on Equity and Access in Higher Education, Derrick and Griffin (1993: 101) stressed that current tertiary systems alienate disadvantaged students from their own cultures and leave them in a position where they are unable to adequately participate in the mainstream culture. They believe university equity programs need to aim to enrich the lives of the students and give them opportunities to enrich the lives of those around them, rather than the reverse. Through examining the progress of this small group of students to their current positions as leaders in student politics, it is hoped that some light may be shed on the successful practices of the Q-Step Programme that can lead to empowerment of this kind.

Context

The Q-Step Programme at QUT was established in 1991 to promote and assist tertiary entrance for students from low socio-economic backgrounds. This cohort, identified by the 'Fair Chance For All' government white paper (1990:2) as being seriously under-represented at tertiary level, is still a major target group of QUT's Student Equity Plan (2000). A commissioned report of the National Board of Employment, Education and Training (1994:24) stated that the processes by which educational disadvantage is socially constituted are 'starkly evident in the institutional context of universities which have traditionally been saturated by elitist values' and that 'obstacles to effective participation continue after students have gained entry to the university. Students worry that they may be misfits in the university environment even after they have the opportunity to enrol.' The need for commencing tertiary students to establish strong peer networks and to 'find one's niche within the institution as a prerequisite to persistence at college' has been explored by Tinto (1987: 58). Specifically in relation to disadvantaged minority students, he states that such students 'face distinct problems in seeking to become incorporated into the life of what may be seen as a foreign community' (1987:161), pointing out that virtually all such students are the first members of their families to enter college. The National Board of Employment, Education and Training (1994) also cites studies demonstrating that 'social isolation and separation from existing social networks' have been nominated by socio-economically disadvantaged students as structural barriers which impede effective participation. McNamara (1995:7), in a paper delivered to the Second National Conference on Equity and Access in Tertiary Education, stated that students must have the belief 'I deserve to be here' in order to successfully access support resources.

Around 200 students enrol annually through the Q-Step Programme. Their university experience commences with a tailored orientation programme which is constantly refined through student input to try to balance information, learning and social activities. An emphasis on team-building helps to create a supportive peer group for students, most of whom come from families with little experience of university. 'Veteran' Q-Step students are always relied on to assist throughout the orientation and their presence, as role models, advisers and guides, is a key factor in the success of the event. Building on the orientation programme, the Q-Step Students Association (QSA) offers an empathic social peer group. It is a student-run social and academic support group, now a formal society of the Student Guild, maintaining the social links developed during the orientation event. The elected President of the organisation is an ex-officio member of the Q-Step Committee, contributing a student perspective to Q-Step policy development. The orientation and membership of the QSA are generally the keys to a smooth transition process for Q-Step students and underpin the sense of belonging for many. Annual participant evaluations of the orientation programme suggest that the events provide a positive introductory experience of QUT and the knowledge that there is support available, if it should ever be needed.

Continuing students figure strongly in all Q-Step activities. Among the values they add to the various initiatives are:

- empathy with the client group and an understanding of the problems they face;
- the personal experience of transition into the university culture;
- a knowledge of the university's operations and ways of dealing with the learning process and the bureaucracy;
- advice based on shared experience.

Utilising continuing Q-Step students is vital to most aspects of the programme's operations. Students who take part in recruitment events are invaluable to the programme, but are also empowering themselves. Many students have overcome initial reserve and humility to speak to groups of school students and others about their experiences as tertiary students. At the Q-Step orientations, as well as being on hand as guides and volunteer workers, continuing students form a welcoming committee, meeting the new arrivals at the registration desk. They also make up a student panel, providing advice in response to questions from the new intake. The encouragement of peers at subsequent Q-Step weekend camps has successfully aided many at-risk students to remain at university and to contribute their own experiences to later events. As with many peer-mentor schemes, the Q-Step peer-mentor programme, based on experience rather than superior course performance, has produced academic benefits for both the mentors and their mentorees. Q-Step's major outreach projects engage Q-Step students as advisers to the high school student participants and a number of Q-Step students are now also employed by QUT's mainstream recruitment unit in the recently established Student Ambassador program. Students have also been encouraged and supported to take part in relevant national and international conferences. One of the major benefits for Q-Step students resulting from participation in these schemes and experiences has been reported to Q-Step staff as an increase in self-esteem. As the students work through their experiences in describing them to others, they are able to see how they themselves have progressed in their journey as students and how they have developed in maturity and confidence. Some have reported a marked flow-on effect to their improved academic progress.

Case studies

Each of the five students in this case study completed a questionnaire and attended a personal interview for the purpose of the study. They have read and given approval to this document.

Four of the case study students, all around twenty years of age, entered QUT directly from high school whilst the fifth entered the university as a mature age student having been in the workforce for some thirty years. All had requested special consideration of socio-economic disadvantage to enter their chosen courses and therefore received the support of the Q-Step Programme. Insufficient time to study, inadequate resources and study space and distance from essential learning resources were quoted as educational problems the students faced in their senior schooling. Added to this were lack of encouragement (two respondents), lack of understanding (two respondents) and peer pressure to avoid studying. Two students also specified the lack of money for school expenses. All five students are from low income or working class families. The mature age student (Bob) is a sole parent to two children and the only one of this group with dependants. Two of the respondents (Julie-Ann and Jackie) are from non-English speaking backgrounds. One of the students has siblings who had attended university but none have tertiary-educated parents. Three claim the encouragement they received from their families to apply for university was weak to non-existent.

School experience for the mature age student ended before Year 12 but all the others completed their schooling. One of these, however, had four changes of high school including working through the School of Distance Education in her final year. All attended State schools serving low income areas. Only one (Susan) attended high school in a country area. Class sizes in Year 12 varied for these students, with Year 12 numbers as high as 120 and as low as 20 students.

Four of the five students state that high achieving students were ostracised by their Year 12 peers but only two put themselves in this category. In all cases, less than 50% of their peer final year students applied for university entrance, to the best of their knowledge. All the respondents described the attitudes of teachers as 'positive' and three stated that school staff were major influences on their decisions to apply for university. Only one of the respondents listed their family as an influence in this regard. None of the students had membership of a political party or any experience in political areas prior to enrolling at QUT and had received no encouragement from family, friends or school to become politically active.

The case study students are enrolled in a variety of disciplines at QUT. These are Social Science, Secondary Education, Arts/Law and Media Studies. They are all full-time students. All but one have moved away from home to attend university, although it should be noted that one of the school-leaver students has received no family support since Year 10.

Of the five students, Susan holds the most powerful position on the Guild executive. As Welfare Director, she is in charge of an area that has run nine campaigns this year. Susan's working week is at least 24 hours and sometimes up to forty hours during the semester breaks. Becoming an elected student leader has fulfilled an ambition for Susan who had wanted to be school captain in her final year of high school. She says that dream went unfulfilled as popularity played the most important role in the elections. She felt as Welfare Director she would be in a position to provide real and direct help to students. Susan is in the fourth year of a five-year double degree.

Bob is the Guild's Campus Director for QUT's smallest campus. He says this means he does everything. His life experience greatly enhances his competence in his position and he has become a familiar figure to students on that campus. Bob, who is a second-year student, is known around the campus as the person to contact for advice and assistance on student affairs and has become a de facto counsellor as well as Q-Step Programme contact. As a mature age student and a parent, Bob has perspectives on Guild matters that help balance views of some of the younger members. His university life includes an active part in the Q-Step Programme as an executive member of the Q-Step Students Association.

Julie-Ann job-shares her Executive role as Women's Services Director. She is experiencing some difficulty as the junior member of the job-share but her cultural background is an asset and she can identify with non-English speaking background students. Like Susan, Julie-Ann is enjoying a new-found respect among her peers having felt inferior and shy at school. Her tasks involve 'anything that affects women on campus' for which she has a small budget and two part-time officers. Julie-Ann is in her third year of a four-year full-time course.

Jackie is in her third year of full-time study. She edits the Student Guild's newspaper, 'Utopia', and has an additional role as Campus Director for the large city campus. Her dual role provides her with opportunities to observe, report and participate in most aspects of the Guild's functioning. Jackie is paid for 21 hours a week but she finds this often extends to thirty-five hours a week at peak times. Unlike the other four students, Jackie's siblings have attended university. In fact, Jackie is the third member of her family to participate in the Q-Step Programme and is also a member of the Q-Step Students Association executive.

Cathy considers herself to be something of a 'gopher' in her position as Student Services Coordinator. Her brief extends across other portfolios and helps to provide her with a good overview of the Guild's functioning. Cathy, like Susan and Julie-Ann, has not previously been in a position where she is seen as 'influential' and is enjoying having inside knowledge to share with other students. She works a ten-hour week for the Guild and has a second job in a local factory. Cathy is a third year student studying full-time in a four-year education degree and is an executive member of the Q-Step Students Association.

Interview analysis

Initial involvement

All the students expressed a desire to help others and an interest in social justice issues as motivating factors in standing for election to the Guild. 'The opportunity to help make a difference for other students' is a common theme among the group. Only Susan had any active interest in party politics although they nearly all concede a leaning to the political left. Cathy thought it was 'time to stop complaining' and to do something pro-active whilst Julie-Ann decided it was 'time to come out of my shell'.

A key factor for each of the group in moving from interested bystander to election candidate was knowing a Guild executive member who encouraged them to attend a meeting. The Guild's General Secretary at that time was also a Q-Step student and very active within the Q-Step Programme. That student invited some of the group to a Labour Party student caucus. Other members of the group met the same student at the caucus meeting and were encouraged by him to stand for election.

The Q-Step Programme played an essential role for all the students in introducing them to the work of the Guild at Orientation and in presenting them with a role model in the General Secretary. As important, Q-Step gave each of them a sense of belonging and identification with a cohort that they were able to represent. As Bob stated, 'Q-Step gave me the confidence to believe there is a place for everyone at uni. I had a group with which to identify and the strength of the sense of belonging'. Cathy explained that 'the social connections made through the Q-Step were the link. I am a shy person, so I probably would not have made social connections without Q-Step. I met people at orientation and that created a sense of belonging and connectedness'. Susan also spoke of being able to identify with other Q-Step students. 'It provided me with exposure to people like myself,' she said, 'and I wouldn't have known about the numbers of students in this position. It helped me get involved, from an ideological perspective, knowing the position and difficulties of low SES (sic) students.' When asked if she would have run for election if she had not been in Q-Step, Julie-Ann replied 'probably not, but seeing (the General Secretary) at Q-Step meetings and how he helped people made me think how I'd like to do that'. Jackie also cited the General Secretary's influence, stating that she thought 'if he can do it, so can I.' She believes the familiar faces from the Q-Step orientation 'made it more exciting' and gave them confidence. Three of the group became friends at the Q-Step orientation. Having a common interest in social justice and a shared background in the Q-Step Programme gave some cohesion to their goals.

Results of participation

Between them, the students have achieved a considerable amount during this year so far for QUT students. They have been instrumental in introducing many new initiatives including:

- changing the policy on childcare fees to reflect the needs of low income and part-time students
- introducing a number of $200 text book bursaries for low income students
- creating a parent room on campus
- establishing a 'discussion and coffee corner' on one of the campuses to promote social and philosophical debate
- establishing a mature age students' club
- organising a first aid course

- establishing a 'queer department' (sic) within the Guild
- organising a self-defence course and a car maintenance course for women
- provision of a $10,000 budget to assist fee relief for low income students.

Cathy believes that the presence of the Q-Step students in the Guild's executive 'makes sure that the Guild doesn't lose sight of equity as the basic reason for its existence. If equality existed, the Guild wouldn't be necessary'. The others have similar views and their achievements demonstrate the impact they have had on an organisation that Jackie stated 'can sometimes be too political for its own good'. She describes the Guild as being run by 'the Old Guard, mostly people from private school, elite backgrounds' who were reluctant to test new ideas or new approaches to things that had been tried before. 'The Q-Steppers brought in new perspectives,' she said. Bob tends to agree with this view and believes he and the other Q-Step students are able to act as a catalyst in creating a more inclusive Guild, reflecting the broader student make up rather than party political views. Susan is cautiously optimistic that they can gradually change attitudes within the Guild by 'slowly hammering away'.

The students have specific goals they would like to achieve during their terms in office, such as the creation of departments dealing with indigenous students' issues and the needs of students with disabilities. More importantly though, for all the group, the change they would most like to introduce is greater inclusiveness. As Cathy puts it, 'I'd like to see us bring more "normal" students into the Guild, not just the politically-motivated'. She sees the skills and ideas of the total student body as a vast resource that generally goes to waste. More people from the same background as the Q-Step students would help to change the Guild, according to Cathy. Jackie agrees this would lead to a more 'cooperative, inclusive approach, exploring issues more deeply rather than rejecting ideas just on party politics'. All the students have identified many benefits accruing to the Guild, the University and themselves through their participation. On a personal level, they all agree on the increase in their confidence and self-esteem. Julie-Ann says she was unable to speak in public before taking on her role in the Guild. 'I'm more "out there",' she says. 'I'm more confident, especially in public speaking.' Jackie has also become more outspoken and more aware of 'how the bureaucratic system works, how to play the game and how to survive'. She has increased her public relations skills and made useful contacts including politicians and students of other universities. Cathy feels better informed about a wide range of social issues of which she had only surface knowledge previously and believes this not only helps her now but will be of great benefit in her future teaching career as she will be able to understand and give better help to her students with their particular issues. Bob sums up the experience by saying 'uni experience without the Guild is not empowering – with it, it can give you back a sense of personal power – you hand over a lot of power to the university when you first enrol. The Guild provides a forum for testing that personal power'.

Academically, most of the group claim to have increased their academic skills if not their grades. Having the confidence 'to converse with academics on equal terms' has given Julie-Ann help with her own studies. Bob has maintained his grades but Jackie says she has let her grades drop slightly as she has put Guild issues first. Susan says she has been 'forced to get the balance right' in her life with so many things competing for her time, and this has led to an improvement in academic performance. Cathy has also had to become more organised. She says her 'grades improved as I was forced to take time out to look at issues and plan ahead, not just the week before due dates, and so I had to research earlier and be more specific as to what information I needed to find'.

All the group recommend the Guild experience for other low income students. According to Bob, it opens up a lot of possibilities but it is essentially an empowering exercise. 'Q-Step students,' he says, 'should be active members of everything they do, not passive consumers.' Cathy stresses that their involvement need not be political and that new students should take an active interest in the Guild and find out about the real issues. One of those 'real issues' for Jackie is where the Student Guild fees go and making the Guild more accountable. Julie-Ann agrees that Guild involvement benefits new students in that they 'make great contacts and gain increased confidence'. Susan believes students should 'find their feet' before becoming too involved in the Guild. She says, though, 'it's enjoyable being involved in things that really interest you and that you can have a hand in doing something about. It may improve your grades and it definitely improves the quality of the student experience'.

Part of the 'value added' experience for these students is the opportunity to serve on university committees and boards, particularly the University Academic Board (UAB). This Board has thirty-eight members, mostly senior academics, and includes six undergraduate student representatives. The Guild executive attend on a rotational basis but, according to Bob, there is always at least 50% Q-Step student representation. Susan finds the Board intimidating due to the environment and the seniority of the academic members and has noted some subtle intimidation being used to censor discussion, but is confident in her role and ability to inject a fresh perspective into the debates. Cathy says there is a need to 'constantly make small statements to get noticed' and that the Q-Step students bring 'a focus on equity - more diversity, which means great ideas which would be lost without equity'.

Recommendations for action

From the students' statements can be drawn recommendations relevant to the Q-Step Programme's strategic planning. These reflect the need to continue and to reinforce those aspects of the Programme's support activities that lead to personal empowerment of the students. For instance, the Q-Step Students Association (QSA) was seen as instrumental in strengthening the 'sense of belonging' as it aids identification with the cohort and provides the social contacts necessary for the students to feel supported by and representative of a recognised student group. Strengthening the QSA through increasing its exposure at orientation and greater promotion of its activities through the official Q-Step newsletters should help ensure a healthier organisation. As Bob said, there is strength in the sense of belonging. Competent role models are seen as essential, as demonstrated by the strong influence that one Q-Step student has had on the interview group. That student, who had been President of the QSA then General Secretary of the Student Guild, was always willing to speak at Q-Step events, encouraging full participation in all aspects of university life, especially in Q-Step and QSA activities. Members of the interview group will participate in forthcoming orientation activities and a proposed 'buddy system' as positive and successful role models and advisers. It was Jackie who suggested a 'buddy system' be introduced at orientation, in which interested new students link up with Q-Step/Guild members to explore how the Guild and student politics work at QUT. This could include workshops at orientation and work-shadowing at appropriate times during the academic year. Encouragement, and possibly financing by the Guild and Q-Step, to attend student conferences could also be a part of this system. Collaboration between the Q-Step Programme and the Guild is a natural extension of current activities. As well as jointly financing student participation at relevant conferences, consideration should be given to joint research projects involving Q-Step staff, Q-Step students and the Guild's Education and Welfare Directors. Topics relevant to the cohort, such as the introduction of full-fee post-graduate courses, childcare and the costs imposed by new technologies, have been suggested as starting points for such collaborative investigations.

Another suggestion was for a series of workshops to be established to help students who participate in university committees become more familiar with committee procedure. A greater understanding of the procedure may help empower students on committees such as the Academic Board. Susan had described some of the intimidating practices and, at times, dismissive manner, of those in powerful positions in such committees. Guild members and staff of the QUT Equity Office (which already runs such courses for female university staff on committees) could jointly implement a seminar series which would include empowering strategies for the Q-Step students. Throughout their student life, Q-Step students should be given greater incentive to participate as active consumers of the educational and social processes of which they are a part. This requires more than the information and encouragement currently provided at orientation and other Q-Step events and should be another area for joint consideration by the Q-Step Programme and the Student Guild. Students are already overloaded with information, therefore careful consideration needs to be given as to how to inform students in a meaningful way of methods to interact positively with staff, become aware of their rights and responsibilities and make the most of their time at university.

Conclusion

The interview group were unanimous in stressing the personal empowerment they have gained from active participation in student politics. They believe the personal benefits make the sacrifices (of time and social life) worthwhile. The development of contacts, a deeper understanding of general politics, a better understanding of the university, increased academic performance, increased confidence and the ability to make changes for the benefit of other disadvantaged students are a few of the benefits listed by the interview group that have added value to their university experience. There is a sense of frustration common among the group that party politics diminish the potential performance of the Guild. They do, however, see themselves as being in a position to introduce reforms to create a more inclusive executive.

The students' comments have given an insight into the motivating factors and supportive influences that have prompted them to become involved in student leadership and to act as advocates for the group with which they identify. They share an intrinsic desire to help others from similarly disadvantaged backgrounds and to give voice to their needs and it was this that attracted each of them to some initial involvement in Guild activities. The students have been able to identify an electorate within the Q-Step cohort. Through involvement in a range of activities presented by the Q-Step Programme, they have developed a strong sense of belonging in an otherwise unfamiliar environment. The students' observations have underscored the need for the support, such as the targeted orientation and the social activities of the Q-Step Students Association, provided through the Q-Step Programme. More importantly, they have provided a number of practical recommendations to expand and reinforce the empowerment of the Q-Step cohort. Their recommendations for additional empowering strategies will be implemented at subsequent Q-Step orientations. These will be carefully monitored as part of the next stage of this work-in-progress.

This case study has shown that these students feel empowered to operate within the mainstream political culture of the university even though they identify with a marginalised, non-traditional cohort. They feel they are in a position make an immediate impact on some of the practices of QUT and that the building blocks are in place to establish a strong and positive force for systemic change in which the needs of the least advantaged are a normal feature of planning. Outcomes such as positive changes to childcare policies, the provision of a fee relief system for socio-economically disadvantaged students and responding to the identified needs of other minority groups on campus demonstrate what can be achieved in a relatively short time by an empathic and committed group. Programmes like Q-Step are in a strong position to help bring about such desirable institutional change through providing the empowering information, advice and social structures necessary for students from non-traditional backgrounds. This structured support assists non-traditional students to maintain their sense of identity whilst integrating into the mainstream of student life. In this way, the students are empowered to make a very valuable contribution to the university as leaders whilst enhancing their own student experience.

References

Atweh, B, and Bland, D (1999), Beyond participation towards social justice: The SARUA Project, *Widening Participation and Lifelong Learning*, vol.1, No.1, pp. 27-33.

Bland, D. (1998) 'Breaking out and breaking in: a multi-faceted system of support for socio-economically disadvantaged students', *First Year in Higher Education Conference Proceedings,* Third Pacific Rim Conference, Auckland, New Zealand.

Department of Employment, Education and Training (1990) *A Fair Chance for All: Higher Education that's within Everyone's Reach*, Canberra, AGPS.

Derrick, M. and Griffin, H. (1993) 'Transforming the system or transforming the disadvantaged: Higher education equity in the 1990s', *First National Conference on Equity and Access in Higher Education Conference Proceedings*, Newcastle (NSW), Australia.

Equity Section (1998), *Equity Plan (1999-2003)*, Brisbane, QUT Publications.

Higher Education Council (1996). *Equality, Diversity and Excellence: Advancing the National Higher Education Equity Framework*, National Board of Employment, Education and Training, Canberra: AGPS.

McInnis, C. and James, R. with McNaught, C. 1995, First year on campus: diversity in the initial experiences of Australian undergraduates, Committee for the Advancement of University Teaching, Melbourne.

McNamara, E. A. (1995), 'Researching best practice in the provision of academic support for equity students', *Second National Conference on Equity and Access in Tertiary Education*, Melbourne.

Silver, H. and Silver, P. (1997) *Students: Changing Roles, Changing Lives*, Open University Press, Buckingham.

Terenzi, P.T., (1992) 'The transition to college project: Final Report', *Out-of Class Experiences Research Program*, National Centre on Post-Secondary Teaching, Learning and Assessment, University Park: Pennsylvania State University, pp. 26-28.

Tindle, E. (1995) 'On becoming an undergraduate: transition to university', *First Year Experience – Conference Proceedings*, Pacific Rim Conference, Melbourne.

Tinto, V. (1987) *Leaving College: Rethinking the Causes and Cures of Student Attrition*, Chicago: University of Chicago Press.

Chapter Fifteen

FUTURE TRANSFORMED: participation in the study of fine art by mature students

Kate Hughes and Anthony Heywood

This chapter presents a case study of a specialised degree programme in Fine Art. This particular programme is part time, and was set up, over ten years ago, to specifically increase the participation of mature students previously denied educational opportunity. We briefly outline the history of part time degree provision in Britain, and then examine the anomalies that exist in fine art education. These are principally that it does not have an immediately obvious commercial application, and that it is frequently regarded as elitist. This chapter describes how marketing, collaboration, learning support and curriculum delivery have all evolved to help dispel these notions, and also meet the very particular needs of widely diverse students. Besides examining these changes, their outcomes and how future policy should proceed, we also include a brief study of added value. Each cohort was divided into qualified and unqualified at the point of entry and then degree classifications. The conclusion summarises the contribution the programme has made to lifelong learning and suggests other ways forward.

The chapter evaluates the attempts to widen access to, and participation in, a programme of study which leads to a BA (Hons) in Fine Art. This is a case study of a particular part time programme which lasts five years. It has much in common with part-time provision in the rest of the UK in that all its students are mature, they are predominantly women, and they have diverse educational backgrounds. Where it differs from the usual is that this programme takes place at the Canterbury site of the Kent Institute of Art & Design on a relatively small campus (816 students) which offers highly specialised study in Fine Art and Architecture, and therefore appeals to a very specific student.

Fine Art does not have a positive image. The British have never been noted for their appreciation of the visual arts and we live increasingly in a society where the pursuit of a study which is perceived to be of little commercial use is not encouraged. When the media focus on Fine Art it is usually to ridicule what are regarded as the excesses of contemporary practice, which does not encourage public confidence in the rigours of a Fine Art degree.

The tabloids have long encouraged derision at non-representational art, and have positively relished the more recent offerings of the Young British Artists, from pickled sharks to dishevelled beds. Reservations are also voiced, albeit with less exuberance, by the broadsheets. A recent article in the Independent – (David Lister 2001) reports on an exhibition at Tate Modern which features a selection of Tracey Emin's underwear. The writer refers, with barely concealed disparagement, to the artist's 'smalls' and then notes, somewhat disingenuously on these items, that 'artistically they are deemed to form part of an exhibition of the London Scene'. We now know that students on our course rapidly learn to evaluate these observations and this is frequently the basis of student debate. This was not so obvious when the course was first mooted. Despite this, there was sufficient determination on the Canterbury Campus to go ahead with a programme of part-time provision.

The programme was validated in 1989, a sufficient time span to identify effective strategies, evaluate performance, and, thankfully, to celebrate considerable achievement in reaching those who never thought that their deep affinity with the visual arts could be realised through degree level study. But before examining this particular programme it might be beneficial to begin with a general survey of part-time higher education in the UK.

Part-time study is convenient, it is relatively cheap and it has undoubtedly widened access. The most recent figures from HESA (HESA April 2000) for academic year 1998/99 show that for UK postgraduates the number of part-timers was about 2.5 times the number of full timers (223,744 compared with 90,818). The corresponding figures for undergraduates were 398,938 part-timers compared with 912,972 on full time programmes, i.e. the number of part-timers was equivalent to about 44% of full time students. These figures represent a large increase in the part-time student population in recent years.

Because of the reasons already mentioned, art and design education has not been in the forefront of part time education. The largest programmes are in subjects allied to medicine (including nursing), engineering and technology, business and administrative studies, and education. In all these subjects, with the exception of engineering and technology, there is a preponderance of women [see Table 1].

Table 1 – All part-time students by Gender 1997-98

	Total	Female	Male
United Kingdom	592989	331570	261419
Other European Union	14064	6712	7352
Other Overseas	26884	11296	15588
Non-UK sub-Total	40948	18008	22940
Total	633937	349578	284359

Source: *HESA 1998*

Yet despite this massive growth it is remarkable that relatively little attention has been paid to the development of part time study, and, as a corollary, the H.E. sector as a whole has not engaged in a policy debate on this issue. A recent conference on how to encourage participation and achievement by mature students was of interest and value but it did not concern itself with the highly specific problems of part time study (CVCP Conference Oct 2000). The growth of part-time provision is largely attributable to the national Open University, which provides part time study by distance learning, and, during the 70s and 80s to some of the large polytechnics who established courses that usually ran alongside full time provision. This undoubtedly widened access, but largely for the exceptionally self-motivated who regretted lost educational opportunities and had the confidence and determination to go for a second chance.

Things changed in 1992 when the binary line was abolished and the polytechnics and some of the larger colleges were re-styled as universities. Although hierarchical and institutional divisions still existed, and in some areas still do, this new classification undoubtedly pushed the "old" universities towards part time provision. The number of qualified full time students were almost all catered for, therefore the established universities had to look to part time students to meet quotas and growth targets. A related issue was the withdrawal of funds from old style liberal adult education in favour of award bearing courses. All institutions pushed towards certificated and credit bearing provision. There was, therefore, a conscious policy to reach out to those members of the community who had not previously considered higher education, and access provision was duly expanded to facilitate these potential students.

Obstacles in the way of part-time learning

The contention of this chapter is that despite all these efforts, and the subsequent growth in part time student numbers, more effective strategies need to be implemented to recruit and retain part time mature students, and most crucially to make these students part of a broader educational process. This must include sounder evaluation of the contribution to lifelong learning, and this cannot be judged solely on the basis of dropout rates. The student who grimly perseveres with the programme for the sake of a qualification may well have achieved a personal goal, but the real contribution to life long learning must be positive and transferable learning skills and the confidence that goes with this. We have students who lack formal educational qualifications but have changed the status of their employment while on the course. During the last academic year (1999/2000) a student who was a sales assistant at a well known high street store felt that the course had given her sufficient confidence to apply to become a window dresser. Her application was successful and because of this she was transferred to a large metropolitan branch. She completes her degree in two years time and maintains she will then be ready for another career change. This is an example of the experience which the under represented must acquire in order to become part of an encompassing and ongoing educational experience which should characterise learning in the new millennium.

Looking at the sector in general, there is still a long way to go. Part-time students are often under represented when they reach the institutions of their choice. It is also important to remember that part time students do not have a wide range of options. They are usually restricted geographically, and have to select an institution which is reasonably accessible. Yet an influx of students from the local community can in fact prove to be a valuable asset to the institution, and this is particularly true of the Kent Institute. Many of these students either have links with the community, or forge them as the course progresses and they gain the confidence to approach potential sponsors, and initiate or strengthen relationships with industry or relevant organisations or individuals. These students also constitute the backbone of the increasingly important alumni associations. Yet, despite these positive attributes, and the clear prospect of future benefits, too many part time students are still regarded as peripheral, their status unresolved even by administrators. As Pat Davies has presciently pointed out, part-time higher education is invariably counted as a fraction of full-time [Davies, 1999]. An obvious point, but this can, and frequently does, convey the impression that institutions regard part time as a diluted version of the accepted, and more desirable, mode of full time study. Another problem is that staff, both academic and administrative, frequently find part time mature students 'difficult': a theme that was recurrent at the previously mentioned conference on mature students. Many of these students have had life experiences which make them articulate and confident, many others have had life experiences that were not so positive, but are still characterised by the determination to proceed and succeed in a chosen area of study. The tenacity of these students should be acknowledged, and sometimes applauded, it should not result in marginalisation. Because of the intermittent nature of part time study it is relatively easy to deflect or diffuse complaints. The students are often geographically dispersed, and, when away from the campus they are distracted or consumed by other problems or considerations, either from employers or from domestic circumstances. In these situations it is too easy for part time students to feel that they have little influence or leverage and that they are peripheral to the institution. We discovered in the early days of our own programme that once this perception takes hold it is extremely difficult to dispel. Such a perception is not conducive to social inclusion, or an adequate preparation for lifelong learning. A higher education system which facilitates mass access, may fail its students in every sense, if there is not an adequate framework of support and a "rapid action force" to deal with a student grievance which must be quickly addressed. Without such mechanisms, i.e. regular meetings, easy access to staff and clear channels of communication, the part time student can rapidly feel disenfranchised.

Financial charges

Another sizeable obstacle in the way of part time learning is the inequitable provision of financial support. Part-time students are accustomed to making significant financial contribution to the cost of their studies. These are substantially lower than that of the full time student, and this has led to some internal subsidisation of part-time study which has, in some instances, contributed to the further marginalisation of part-time students particularly on the part of administrators. Yet as Malcolm Tight observed in 1994, 'With the development of modular courses and credit transfer arrangements, and the increasing pressure on students to earn a supplementary income while they are studying, it is doubtful if the financial distinctions between part-time and full-time study can be maintained'. [Tight, 1994] This has proved to be the case. Figures released by Barclays Bank [The Times, April 11, 2000] reveal that the average full time student leaves university bearing a degree, and a debt of £5,286. Barclays also estimate that 80% of students work in vacations, and 40% have term time jobs. Credit accumulation and transfer increasingly allows students to opt in and out of their studies. Tight believes that the British system will become more akin to the North American model with costs and charges based on distinction which will radically change the status of part time students. This possible change does not appear to be either acknowledged or anticipated by many of our institutions.

From 2001, part-time students will be eligible for student loans, which will give them financial parity with full time students. One of the major recommendations contained in the Dearing Report (Dearing, 1997) was that lifelong learning would be further encouraged if part time students did not have a more onerous financial burden than full time students. This is good news for part-time students. Parity with full-time students will also allow the part-time student access to other benefits hitherto denied. This is crucial to the recruitment and progress of the under represented. To take an obvious example: full time students who suspect that they might be dyslexic have access to testing for learning difficulties and are entitled to support . It could be argued that the need is greater for mature students who probably passed through primary and secondary education at a time when learning difficulties were not even acknowledged, let alone recognised. The Hardship Funds (formerly Access) which are funded by HEFCE have also been extended to part time students.

The course at Canterbury

The part time BA at the Kent Institute of Art & Design at Canterbury began in 1989, at a time when higher education in the UK was still structured in the binary system. The Kent Institute was, and is, one of the few monotechnics remaining in the UK, and is spread over three campuses, each one of which is specialist in a particular aspect of Art & Design. Fine Art education in Canterbury, which first began in 1868, has always attracted students from a wide range of social and educational backgrounds. There have been many changes, particularly during the 1970s when Fine Art assumed degree status, but there have always been anomalies in fine art education. The degree course is invariably preceded by a foundation year, making the full time course four years rather than the three that is usual in British universities. In order to maintain parity it was decided that the part time programme would last for five years and students would be encouraged to do a part time Access Course lasting one year. Access provision has proved to be the bedrock of the course. Its crucial function is that it provides an immediate framework in which students from a diversity of backgrounds can come together. Because of the profile of our catchment area, we have a very wide social mix of students. This

Access experience is invaluable in that it inducts those without formal educational qualifications into a rigorous academic structure which we hope is both supportive, unintimidating and, above all, encouraging. Another process which is begun during Access is that of encouraging students to stringently re-examine, and perhaps discard, previously held notions about art and its practices. This is hard for all students, but is probably particularly difficult for those students from relatively deprived backgrounds who have not been in the habit of going to exhibitions of contemporary work or reading reviews in the broadsheets. It is counted as one of the successes of the course that these differences are swiftly resolved, and all students quickly gain the confidence to visit exhibitions and articulate their experiences. As mentioned earlier, fine art has always occupied a unique, and sometimes isolated, position in British society and, therefore, in higher education. It is sometimes shunned for not being sufficiently vocationally orientated, or avoided for being elitist, rarefied or impractical. These are the preconceptions that had to be challenged when establishing a course dedicated to combining the academic rigour of fine art with the individual life skills and experiences of each student. [see Figures. 1, 2 & 3]

Figure 1 - Christine Rothschild, Degree Show 2000
Figure 2 – Debbie Bennett, Degree Show 2000
Figure 3 – Jill Kirby, Degree Show 2000

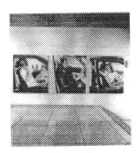

Figure 1

Figure 2

Figure 3

The development of the course

Another potential obstacle to widening access was the lack of societal variables in the region. East Kent is predominantly affluent and white, and students who conform to this pattern have little difficulty in finding their way to our admissions office. The College Campus already has a well-established reputation for curating a variety of first class public exhibitions, but these events do not succeed in attracting those sections of the community who do did not regard higher education in general, or art exhibitions in particular, as a part of their lives. Yet for the proposed course to have the necessary richness and variety, and more pragmatically, to maintain numbers, this was the constituency we had to reach.

It was decided that the most effective way to do this was to target adult education courses specialising in fine art, which were scattered throughout the county and speak directly with potential students and their tutors. The subsequent importance of Access has already been mentioned, but at this stage the potential level of interest or commitment was unknown, and another concern was that many of these centres were a considerable distance from the campus. To students already encumbered with fees, the cost of travelling in both money and time, might well prove a disincentive. Unlike a large metropolitan institution, we do not have an infrastructure of public transport. We discovered that our policy of targeting particular regions ameliorated this problem, in that students could share car journeys. This may seem academically insignificant but it is considerations such as these which, particularly in the early stages of the course, are very important to retaining student numbers. Good relations with adult education therefore became an integral part of our recruitment, and our familiarity with these institutions provided students with a sense of continuity which increased their confidence.

During the last three years two further education colleges with whom we have established a strong and mutually supportive relationship have begun to offer formally accredited qualifications in Fine Art to Certificate or Diploma level. We greatly welcomed this innovation, and encouraged those students who chose this mode of study to come to us for the final stage of the programme, the degree stage. The obvious advantage is that those students whose circumstances would preclude the commitment to five years of travel can often manage the last stage of the degree programme. This development is still in its infancy: this is one of our strategies for widening access that we are seeking to develop.

Our first priority in designing the course was to make the prospect of degree level unintimidating and attainable, our second was to offer a flexibility of provision. The programme which is unitised was divided into three stages, each one concluding in a formally certificated award of Certificate, Diploma or Degree, which is also an exit point. From the beginning we positively encouraged non-conventional entrants and it was envisaged that those students who were not of a sufficiently high standard to proceed to degree level, would be able to leave the course with a recognised qualification, and a positive learning experience. By the time the third cohort had passed the Certificate Stage it became obvious that we had been unduly pessimistic. Once students without formal academic qualifications became confident, their determination and burgeoning ability did the rest. We began to realise a very obvious, but very valuable, lesson: our students are our greatest strength. The programme was therefore gradually amended to promote greater peer group interaction through seminars and discussion, sometimes organised by the students, and taking place in the evening outside scheduled hours. It was during these sessions that students without formal educational qualifications began to slowly but surely realise that they had opinions of equal value and, more importantly, they could substantiate them.

Social and educational background of students

It is difficult to arrive at precise figures for the socio-economic status of our students. The only variables readily available are sex and age [see Table 2]. Data for part time students is not as comprehensive as that for full time, and an added complication is that whereas a full time student's socio-economic status is based on the head of their household, for part time it is based on the student's own employment record. Given that the majority of our students are mature women, a sizeable proportion of whom have devoted themselves to their families rather than actively pursuing a career, it is difficult to arrive at meaningful figures.

Another problem is the particular nature of art education. In their survey of 1997 concerning lifelong learning, Robertson and Hillman are more concerned with those students who entered directly in the labour market instead of HE because this was ordained by "habit, culture and professional or peer expectation" [Robertson, 1997]. A large number of our students do not fit this description. Many, at an earlier stage, were reluctant recruits into a sector of higher education that was deemed by both school and parents to offer better employment prospects. An engineering draftsman wrote on his application form: 'As you will see from my career details I have spent my working life in civil municipal engineering.

Table 2 – Age distribution of first-year UK domiciled undergraduates (1)
by mode of study 1998/98

| | | First Degree | |
	Total	Full-time	Part-time
18 & under	43.6	47.9	1.1
19	18.4	20.1	1.6
20	6.9	7.3	2.6
21-24	11.7	11.2	16.3
25-29	6.8	5.4	21.3
30 & Over	12.6	8.2	57.1
Total	**100.00**	**100.00**	**100.00**

(1) – Those whose age is known   Source HESA 1998, Tables 1b and 1f.

However my one wish in life was to receive formal art training on leaving grammar school but because parental wishes were to the contrary I was not allowed to do so'. Patricia a graduate social worker wrote: 'I studied Fine Art at Nottingham College of Art after leaving school. I left before completing the course due to withdrawal of financial support by my parents'. It was only after the deaths of their respective parents that both these students hesitantly approached the access course. They both achieved first class degrees, maintain contact with the course and appear to be leading fulfilled lives.

The advantage of a small campus which is part of a mono technic is that it provides a positive environment in which to become familiar with the social characteristics of the students, and without being intrusive, be aware of life styles, competing demands and problems. The relative accessibility of staff which a small campus facilitates, and the communal nature of a lot of fine art activity is also of immeasurable value to students whose time on campus is limited. It is strongly felt that this supportive environment plays a very important role in adding value to the programme we offer. Guidance, counselling and learning support are crucial to maintaining student numbers and providing a sound learning base.

Because our students are not only from a wide range of backgrounds, but also have a wide diversity of formal academic achievement, value added is a difficult concept to measure. If we take the gap between entry level, (which includes a high number of non conventional entrants) and the exit level, (the degree level attained by the student) [see Table 3], we can have some measure of value added.

Table 3 – 5 Cohorts PTBA Fine Art, KIAD, 1990-95 to 1994-99

	No.	No with degrees	% with good degrees
Cohort 1, 1990-95			
Underqualified entrants	12	9	75
Qualified entrants	9	5	56
Total	21	14	67
Cohort 2, 1991-96			
Underqualified entrants	8	5	63
Qualified entrants	8	8	100
Total	16	13	81
Cohort 3, 1992-97			
Underqualified entrants	9	4	44
Qualified entrants	11	7	64
Total	20	11	55
Cohort 4, 1993-98			
Underqualified entrants	16	7	44
Qualified entrants	8	6	75
Total	24	13	54
Cohort 5, 1994-99			
Underqualified entrants	10	4	40
Qualified entrants	11	6	55
Total	21	10	48
All 5 cohorts, 1990-95/1994-99			
Underqualified entrants	55	29	53
Qualified entrants	47	32	68
Total	102	61	60

We analysed five cohorts of students and sub-divided each cohort into those who fulfilled conventional academic entry requirements **before access**, and those who were under qualified at this point. The object of this analysis was to see if there was any significant difference between the 'qualified' graduates who obtained good degrees (First or Upper Second), and the "under qualified". The difference was significant in that 68% of qualified and 53% under qualified prior to Access were awarded good degrees, but it is also significant that half of the 'under qualified' gained good degrees.

This figure suggests a high degree of value added for the under qualified. The growth of student centred learning and peer group interaction promotes a healthy and symbiotic learning relationship in that during the early stages formal academic practice interacts with diverse life skills and experiences. The course is five years long which allows each cohort to establish its own identity. It also nurtures friendships and social interaction which would be highly unlikely outside the course. Ideas, aspirations and life experiences are discussed and disseminated both within and without the formal academic framework to the advantage of all students.

Our curriculum has from the outset facilitated flexible learning. As mentioned earlier, this has become a necessity for all courses, largely because of financial pressure. The profile of the part time student (female and 30+) means that the pressures are not only financial. The problems of elderly parents, adolescent children, and often, crucially, the strains which are put on a relationship when one partner becomes more confident, assertive or independent all impact on the course. 27% of our students intermit, and we have established, and more importantly, maintained a supportive academic structure which encourages this flexibility. This is another example of the fact that development in course structure, presentation and assessment has been more prevalent in part time programmes.

There is still a long way to go. Many employers are unwilling to fund part time education in fine art, although we are unusual in that the small number of students [4] who do receive financial support from this source are all women. (Hill, MacGregor 1998). Rules governing unemployment benefit may also work against part time students, and there is the perennial problems of conflicting and compelling interests, not least the financial. Students who are eligible for social security have their fees remitted, and the wider distribution of Hardship Funds has come as a welcome relief to many students. The art student also has the added expense of a continual need for materials, and because of the wide catchment area, travel and subsistence add to the cost of study on this course.

Higher education must involve a balance of different kinds of provision and delivery. The contribution is not only to the economy and manpower plans of society, there are also wider values of socialisation. Higher education as a leisure related investment is relevant, and is, in our experience, not incompatible with, what is regarded as higher education's most vital purpose, that of scholarship. There is genuine danger lurking in a society which prioritises immediate commercial application, and neglects the freedom to explore knowledge. For those who seize learning opportunities later on in life, the pursuit of knowledge and skills can give pleasure to the individual, or, more crucially, be passed on to families. We regard this as particularly important for women students, who begin the course under-qualified and are sometimes from relatively deprived backgrounds. Their achievement and example does provide a positive role model for their families and particularly their daughters. We have had two examples of daughters, who may not have considered Higher Education as an option, but proceeded to follow their mothers on the course.

Conclusion

The texture, diversity, and success of the course is generated maintained, and ultimately renewed by it's students. The initial pace of teaching and learning is set by those students who have had previous experience of Higher Education. They are invariably familiar with terminology, have a relaxed approach to tutors and are eager to engage with new ideas and concepts from the first day.

The study of student achievement previously examined, is an indication of how this balance is ultimately redressed. The non traditional learners have ideals, ideas and convictions which have survived years of isolation and sometimes a high and consistent level of discouragement. Suddenly these secretly cherished and fragile aspirations are legitimised and substantiated. It is this realisation and the opportunities it offers which transforms the insecure and inarticulate into the confident and the positive.

There must be acknowledgement that Higher Education, and, to declare an interest, fine art, enriches lives and makes a major contribution to a society by the preservation of cultural values, and a forward looking and flourishing policy towards the arts. By widening participation and access we firmly believe that we are doing something to work towards this objective. There are still obstacles to overcome and battles to be won, but with every passing academic year we have greater numbers on our side and more futures are transformed.

Reference

Lister, D. – *The Independent – 31 January 2001*

HESA April (2000) *Students in Higher Education Institutions* 1998/99 Tables C&D pp.8-9.

CVCP Conference (Oct 2000) – *Mature Students Encouraging Participation and Achievement.*

Davies, P. (1999) Half full not half empty: A positive look at part-time education *Higher Education Quarterly*, pp.141-155.

Tight, M. (1994) Models of part-time higher education: Canada and the UK. *Comparative Education*, Vol.30, No.3, p.188.

The Times ,Tuesday 11 April 2000.

Robertson, D. (1997) *Higher Education and Lifelong Learning for Social Justice in the Learning Market.* University of Liverpool, p.61.

The Report of the National Committee of Enquiry into Higher Education. (1997) Chaired by Sir Ron Dearing.

Hill, Y. and MacGregor, Support systems for women in part-time study *Journal of Further and Higher Education vol 22 no. 2: June 98 p, 143-149.*